Bas Apologetics For Evangelism

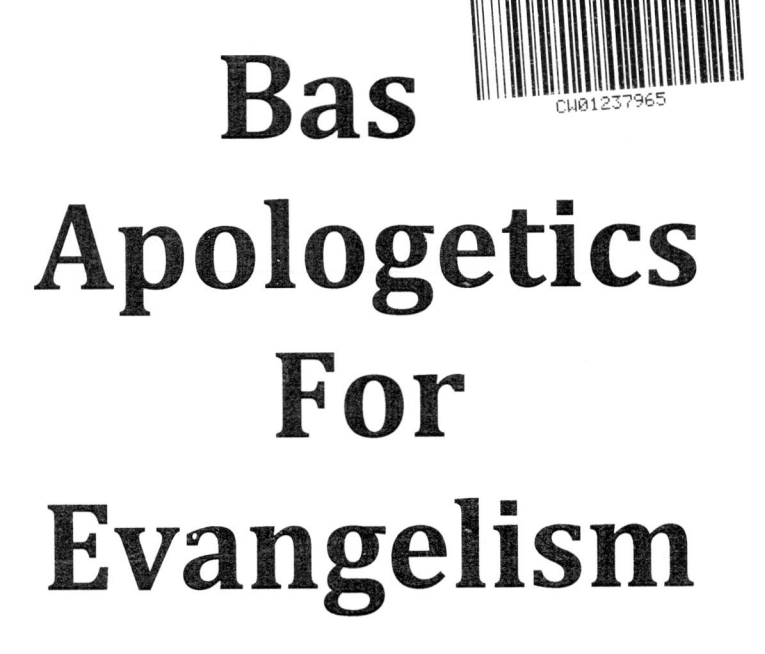

Helping People Find God

Austin Baxter

ACKNOWLEDGEMENTS:

Scripture quotations from the authorised version of the bible (King James Version). The rights which are vested in the Crown, are reproduced by permission of the Crown's Patentee, Cambridge University Press.

This material is copyright and may not be - reproduced in any format, written or electronic without the express permission of the author: Austin Baxter.

Published by:
Spirit of Revival Evangelism
Birmingham
United Kingdom
Copyright 2014

ISBN: 978-0-9928169-3-3

SPIRIT OF REVIVAL EVANGELISM
Tel. No.: 0121 448 2785, MB: 07435 000419
Website: www.spiritandword.org.uk

Contents: Page

Introduction 5

Chapter One: What is Apologetics? 7

- *What is Apologetics?*
- *Why Apologetics in Evangelism?*
- *Different types of Apologetics*

Chapter Two: Introduction to Atheistic Worldviews 23

- *Introduction to Worldviews*
- *Secular Humanism*
- *Evolution Naturalism*

Chapter Three: Introduction to Theistic Worldviews 38

- *The New Atheism*
- *Definition of Islam*

Page

Chapter Four: Responding to Different Worldviews   63

- *Jehovah Witnesses*
- *Responding to Secular Humanism, Evolution, New Atheism*
- *Responding to Muslims*
- *Responding to Jehovah Witnesses*

Bibliography   90

INTRODUCTION

"But sanctify the Lord God in your hearts: and be ready always to give an answer to every man that asketh you a reason of the hope that is in you with meekness and fear:" 1 Peter 3:15

"...it was needful for me to write unto you, and exhort you that ye should earnestly contend for the faith which was once delivered unto the saints." Jude vs. 3

Welcome to this book, Basic Apologetics For Evangelism. This book aims to give you the skills and knowledge to be able to defend your faith in today's secular and anti-Christian culture and society. The Christian Faith is under fierce attack from many quarters. When we do Evangelism we often meet people who are antagonistic to the gospel and have criticisms and arguments against Christianity. We also encounter people who have different beliefs, different worldviews than our own. These people believe that their beliefs are equal and even superior to the Christian message of Salvation through Jesus Christ. Our society and the forces that influence it such as Education and the mass media are against the Christianity and the Bible and want to replace them with a secular humanist worldview and agenda. Britain and Europe have abandoned their traditional Christian heritage and replaced it with Humanism, the new religion of the Western world.

As Christians we have an obligation to preach the Gospel to all men and women whatever their beliefs or persuasion (Mark 15:16). However we cannot ignore the different beliefs, ideas and opinions that people in Britain have today about spiritual issues. When we go out to evangelise, it is not enough to simply preach the Gospel to people. We must address and answer their criticisms about our Faith and challenge their worldviews to show them where they are in error. We must engage in apologetics. Apologetics is the defence of the Christian Faith. It also involves challenging other worldviews and beliefs and showing their inconsistencies and error so as to lead people who hold them into the truth of the Gospel. To evangelise in Britain today we have to do apologetics, we have to first challenge the ideological strongholds that have gripped the minds of men and stop them from seeing the truth of the Gospel (2 Corinthians 4:4, 5:10). Apologetics is pre-evangelism. It is the first step believers have to take before they can share their faith with unbelievers. In evangelism our goal is to save souls. Like the apostle Paul the most effective way to do this is to become all things to all men (1 Corinthians 9:22). Apologetics allows us to get into the minds and hearts of unbelievers when we discuss and challenge their beliefs. The sad truth is that Satan has blinded the hearts and minds of unbelievers through erroneous beliefs and practices (2 Corinthians 4:4). People are lost in a maze of religions and philosophies that have blinded them to the reality of Christ their saviour. A key objective of this book is to equip you the knowledge to help those bound by erroneous beliefs and lead them to the reality and person of Jesus Christ. To do this however, we must first know what people believe and why they believe it. Once we address their beliefs and show people their inherent weaknesses then we can give them the Gospel, and introduce them to truth Himself, the person of our Lord and saviour Jesus Christ (John 14:6).

Austin Baxter
EVANGELIST

Chapter One
What is Apologetics?

"But sanctify the Lord God in your hearts: and be ready always to give an answer to every man that asketh you a reason of the hope that is in you with meekness and fear:" 1 Peter 3:15

"...it was needful for me to write unto you, and exhort you that ye should earnestly contend for the faith which was once delivered unto the saints...." Jude vs. 3

"A dog barks when his master is attacked. I would be a coward if I saw that God's truth is attacked and yet would remain silent."
John Calvin

"If our culture is to be transformed, it will happen from the bottom up - from ordinary believers practicing apologetics over the backyard fence or around the barbecue grill. "
Charles (Chuck) Colson

"False ideas are the greatest obstacles to the reception of the gospel. We may preach with all the fervor of a reformer and yet succeed only in winning a straggler here and there, if we permit the whole collective thought of the nation to be controlled by ideas [...] which prevent Christianity from being regarded as anything more than a harmless delusion."
- J. Gresham Machen

Introduction to Apologetics

Apologetics is the defence of the Christian Faith using rational, historical, moral and scientific arguments to demonstrate that the Christian Faith is truth itself. Apologetics aims to help Christians defend their faith and lead unbelievers to the knowledge of Christ. Apologetics is the rational, logical defence of the Christian Faith against its many opponents. Apologetics is vast field covering many different academic disciplines, philosophy, history, science, morality, the Bible, the Person and Work of Jesus and the question of God's existence. God has raised up men and women, whom He has equipped with the knowledge and skills to defend His word and the truth claims of Christianity. These are the modern day Apologists. Apologetics attempts to do three things. *Firstly* it defends the Christian Faith against the attacks and accusations of its opponents. *Secondly* through rational argument and debate, it attempts to show the inherent weaknesses of other religious and secular worldviews. *Thirdly,* it aims to help men and women lost in the maze of religions and false worldviews to embrace the truth of Christianity and Jesus Christ. Today our Christian Faith is under considerable attack from atheists who deny the existence of God, and other religions and who deny the truth claims of the Bible and the Christianity. We are living in a post Christian society, which has adopted many different worldviews, religions and philosophies about the nature of the world and reality itself. Atheism, Naturalism, Islam, Jehovah Witnesses and many other viewpoints are part of our culture and society. Many Christians encounter atheists, agnostics, humanists, Muslims and Jehovah witnesses, and do not know how to respond to them. When these groups begin to attack their faith, these Christians draw back because they do not know how to respond to their objections. This often results in these people being unconverted and more hardened than ever to the Gospel. The only way Christians can be prepared to deal and respond to these groups of people, is by studying Apologetics. Apologetics will equip you with the knowledge and confidence to defend your Christian Faith.

When we evangelise, we will encounter people who have different views about the world and the universe (a worldview). If we want to help them then we need to know what they believe and why they believe it. Once we have this knowledge then we can demonstrate to our opponents how their worldviews are inadequate explanations for the origin life, mankind and the universe. Once we engage people through apologetics and show the reasonableness of the Christian Faith, God can open a door into their minds and hearts for us to plant the seed of the Gospel into them (Mark 4:14-20). In this book, we will examine the following worldviews, **Secular Humanism, Evolution, the New Atheism, Islam and Jehovah Witnesses.**

Every Believer is an apologist for their Faith.

You may say I do not need Apologetics, I just preach the Gospel. Well whether you are aware of it or not you are already involved in Apologetics. Every Christian who shares and defends their Faith is an apologist. The only question is whether you are a good one or a bad one. Few believers realise that the Bible actually commands us to defend our faith with reasonable and persuasive arguments (1 Peter 3:15). A response that you will often hear when you approach unbelievers today is this: "Since there are so many religions and philosophies out there, how do I know which one is the truth?" In answering this type of question, you will find yourself giving reasons for your Faith, and this is apologetics. God wants us to "study to show ourselves approved" (2 Timothy 2:15) so that when we meet unbelievers, we can show them that we have examined the issues that concern them. In today's secular culture, apologetics is pre-evangelism; you have to engage in it before you can present the Gospel to unbelievers.

Action Point

List down the three tasks of Apologetics

How is apologetics related to evangelism?

What do we mean when we say all believers are apologists?

What is apologetics?

"But sanctify the Lord God in your hearts: and be ready always to give an answer to every man that asketh you a reason of the hope that is in you with meekness and fear." 1 Peter 3:15

A. Definition of the word "apologia"-apologetics

Thayer's Definition[1]
1) verbal defence, speech in defence
2) a reasoned statement or argument

The word "apologia" is found 2 verses of the New Testament. Firstly in Acts 16:2, where Paul say tells King Festus " I make my defence"*(Grk.apologia")* and in 1 Peter 3:15, where Peter tells us we must always be ready to give an answer-Greek "apologia" defence of the Christian faith. It literally means a reasoned defence of something, of one self or one's belief.

A person involved in Christian apologetics is *a defender of Christianity* or *Christian apologist* (*apologete* in older literature). In the English language, the word *apology*, usually refers to asking for forgiveness for a blameworthy act. Christian Apologetics however is not an apology in this sense but is a reasoned defence, of the validity and truth claims of the Christian Faith. Because our Faith is under attack we must obey the scriptural commands to defend the Faith (1 Peter 3:15, Jude vs. 3). This means that as Christians, we must be prepared to enter the public arenas of debate, and present the case for the truth of the Christian worldview.

B. Apologetics is part of the History of the Church

Apologetics has always been a part of the Church's history and tradition. In the early period of the Church's life, around the end of the second century God raised up Christian writers who began to defend the Christian Faith against the opponents of their day. Men such as Aristides, Justin Martyr, Tatian, and Athenagoras used their skills and abilities to defend the Christian Faith against heretics and schismatics. Towards the end of the second century, we see men such as Iraneus Bishop of Lyons who wrote five books against Gnostic heresies. There were other great apologists such as Tertullian, Clemet and Origen who defended the faith. Later on in the sixteenth and seventeenth centuries, we see Christian apologists defending the Faith against the rational and scepticism of the Enlightenment period. John Locke wrote a book entitled "The reasonable needs of Christianity" published in 1685, in which he set out to prove that the order and symmetry of the world and universe pointed to the existence of an all powerful, intelligent God. There were men of the eighteenth century who wrote books to defend the Bible against the critics of their day. Men such as Thomas Sherlock wrote "Trial of the Witnesses of the Resurrection (1729), and Nathaniel Lardner wrote a fourteen volume work entitled "The Credibility of the Gospel History". William Paley (1743 - 1805), wrote his classic work "Natural Theology" in which he demonstrated that the order and complexity of the world clearly proved that there had to be an intelligent mind who created it. Some of the great apologists of the twentieth century include men such as C.S Lewis, Cornelius Van Til, John Warwick Montgomery and Francis Schaeffer. Today God is using hundreds of men to defend the Faith. Some of these men include men such as John Gernster, R C Sproul, Josh McDowell, Dr. William Lane Craig, Norman Geilser, to name but a few. We too are part of the army of apologists God wants to raise up in this hour, to remove the lies and blindness that Satan has put over the minds and hearts of men and women (2 Corinthians.4:4).

C. Apologetics is Spiritual warfare for the minds and hearts of men and women

"In whom the god of this world hath BLINDED THE MINDS OF THEM WHICH BELIEVE NOT, lest the light of the glorious gospel of Christ, who is the image of God, should shine unto them."
2 Corinthains.4:4

"Casting down imaginations, and every high thing that exalteth itself against the knowledge of God, and bringing into captivity every thought to the obedience of Christ..." 2 Corinthians 10:5

"False ideas are the greatest obstacles to the reception of the gospel. We may preach with all the fervor of a reformer and yet succeed only in winning a straggler here and there, if we permit the whole collective thought of the nation to be controlled by ideas [...] which prevent Christianity from being regarded as anything more than a harmless delusion." - *J. Gresham Machen*

Apologetics is spiritual warfare for the hearts and minds of men. Apologetics equips us with the knowledge to be able to remove the intellectual stumbling blocks that Satan has set up in the minds and hearts of men which blind them to the truth of the Gospel (2 Corinthians 4:4, 10:5). There is a cosmic warfare going on for the souls of men and women and it is being waged in the arena of ideas, philosophies and religions. Apologetics is spiritual warfare; it is casting down reasonings and imaginations that have been placed in the minds and hearts of men by the principalities and powers of this age (2 Corinthians 10:4-5, Colossians 2:8). The way into a man's souls is through his mind and belief system. Apologetics equips us with the knowledge and skills to help unbelievers find God. Satan knows that if he can get men to believe a lie, then they will live out that lie and end up in Hell. He has successfully developed philosophies and religions that blind men to the truth claims of the Christian Faith. The scriptures clearly teach us about the nature of the Satan, that he is the deceiver of the whole world (Revelation. 21:9). If you have any doubts about is deceiving power, just look at the thousands of ideologies, beliefs and religions there are in the world, each of them designed to blind the minds of men to the reality of the true God (Ephesians 6:10). Apologetics gives us knowledge to lead people out of the maze of these erroneous ideas that Satan has bound them in. Apologetics is about giving and presenting the truth about the world, God, the Bible, Jesus and the world to come. Apologetics is presenting to unbelievers Biblical truth about God, morality, death, judgement, Heaven and Hell, the true nature of man, and salvation through Jesus Christ (Genesis 1:1, 26, Exodus 20:1-16, Hebrews 9:26, Romans 1:18-21, 1 Corinthians 15:1-5). However, before we reach unbelievers with the truths of the Bible and the Gospel, we must refute and cast down counterfeit ideas lodged in their hearts and minds (2 Corinthians 4:4, 10:4-5) These need to be demolished before an unbeliever will be open to receive the Gospel Message (2 Corinthians 10:5). This is the context of our evangelism in Britain today. We are contending with principalities and powers for the hearts and minds of men so that they can come to Christ. Apologetics is spiritual warfare for the minds and hearts of men and women.

Action Point

Define what the word apologetics means

_____

List down four apologists from Church history

_____

___

What do we mean when we say that Apologetics is spiritual warfare?
___

C. Why Apologetics in Evangelism?

We have already discussed some of the reasons why we need to do Apologetics, but there are several more important points we need to look at. In our day and throughout history, Christianity has been under attack. It is our *duty as Christians to defend the Faith* and keep it pure, so that men and women can hear the pure Gospel and be saved. The following are some other reasons why we need to do apologetics in evangelism.

i. The Bible commands us to defend the Faith

Few Christian realise that the Bible actually commands us to give unbelievers reasons why we believe the Bible. The following scriptures exhort us to do this:

"Walk in wisdom toward them that are without, redeeming the time. Let your speech be always with grace, seasoned with salt, *THAT YE MAY KNOW HOW YE OUGHT TO ANSWER EVERY MAN.*" Colossian 4:5-6

Here the apostle Paul tells us that we are to give answers to the questions unbelievers ask.

"Holding fast the faithful word as he hath been taught, that he may be able by sound doctrine both *TO EXHORT AND TO CONVINCE THE GAINSAYERS.*" Titus 1:9

Paul says that one of the qualifications of a bishop is that he must

be able to convince those who are in error. All unbelievers are in error when it comes to God and the teachings of the Bible.
1 Peter 3:15- we have already examined above, tells us to give a defence of our faith.

"Beloved, when I gave all diligence to write unto you of the common salvation, it was needful for me to write unto you, and exhort you that ye *SHOULD EARNESTLY CONTEND FOR THE FAITH WHICH WAS ONCE DELIVERED UNTO THE SAINTS.*

Jude opens his epistle with a command to believers to earnestly contend for the Faith. This means to strive, struggle for the faith. Why do we need to contend for the Faith?

Satan wants to contaminate the true Gospel message with false doctrines and ideas from the world. Popular TV hosts present their "gospel" and interpretation of Christianity and the teachings of Jesus that include many truths of the Bible. This mixture of truth and error is fatal to the spiritual well being of millions of people who listen and believe these ideas. As Christians we must do our utmost to preserve the truth and purity of the Gospel. When we evangelise and teach unbelievers the true Gospel message we are helping to preserve the true Gospel once delivered to the saints (Judevs3).

ii. To confirm the faith of Christians- Attacks against the Christianity can shake the faith of Christians causing some to lose the Faith

"Now when John had heard in the prison the works of Christ, he sent two of his disciples, And said unto him, *Art thou he that should come, or do we look for another?* Matthew 11:3

"But while men slept, *HIS ENEMY CAME AND SOWED TARES AMONG THE WHEAT*, and went his way." Matthew 13: 25.

Apologetics is necessary to confirm and preserve the faith of Christians. When you evangelise you will find many who were once Christians but no longer follow the Lord. The truth is that Christians doubt the things of God, and some even lose their Faith altogether. This is especially true of those who go to secular universities. In these institutions, many Christians are introduced to scientific and secular ideas that attempt to disprove the Bible and religious claims in general. Your teenage children can lose their faith when they go to university and encounter new ideas that contradict the teachings of the Bible. Some Christians lose their faith because of the temptations and lusts of this world as Demas did (2 Timothy 4; 10).Some loose it through getting involved in wrong doctrine and heresy such as Hymaneus (2 Timothy 2:17-18). And some loose it by listening and receiving the philosophies of this world. In Colossians 2:8 Paul writes:

"Beware lest any man SPOIL YOU THROUGH PHILOSOPHY AND VAIN DECEIT, after the tradition of men, after the rudiments of the world, and not after Christ." Colossians.2:8

The word "spoil" here means: "... to lead away as booty, i.e. (figuratively) seduce:--spoil."[2]

This is exactly what is happening to thousands of Christians today. Through educational institutions, colleges and universities, Christian students are exposed to atheistic and materialistic ideas that challenge the Bible and its teaching, and so they are spoiled, taken away captive and lose their faith. A major reason for this is that these Christians were never taught how to defend their faith; they were never taught Apologetics. It is important to recognise that Satan does not relinquish his attack on you because you are a Christian. He will seek to recapture you through the ideas and philosophies of the world (Colossians 2:8).

If you get nothing else from this book, this point alone is good enough reason for you read it, because it can make the difference between your son/daughter loosing or keeping their* *faith in the future, when they go on into to secular universities*

Examples of Believers losing their Faith

1. Dan Barker (born June 25, 1949-) is a prominent American atheist activist who served as a Christian preacher and musician for 19 years but left Christianity in 1984.

2. Frank Schaeffer (1952-), son of the famous evangelical apologist Francis Schaeffer renounced his faith and is now an agnostic

3. Jerry Dewitt (1944-) a former Pentecostal Evangelist, renounced his faith and became an atheist. He now heads up the Clergy Project an atheist organisation that seeks to help Christians who no longer believe transition from their Christian Faith to atheism

4. Christian Youth who attend Universities in America and England

Perhaps the most tragic example of Christians losing their faith is our young people who leave home and enter secular universities in America and the United Kingdom. Numerous studies and books have been written about the plight of our young people who abandon their faith when they leave home and go onto higher education. Secular universities staff overall are atheists, liberals and socialists who oppose Christianity and the Bible. Many professors and lectures at these institutions make it their goal to ridicule and de-convert evangelical Christians. Faced with the pressure and ridicule from these professors and their peers in the university, many Christian youth renounce their Faith and become apostate. A major reason for this is that these young people were not prepared by their parents or their church youth groups to face the attack and criticism against their faith. They were not taught apologetics.

Some studies in America show that as much as 70-75% of Christian youth leave the church after high school (Barna and USA Today).

The rise of the New Atheism led by Richard Dawkins, Christopher Hitchens, Sam Harris and Daniel Dennet and their crusade to rid the world of religion has permeated many universities forcing young people to compromise their beliefs or face ridicule and persecution for their Faith. Countless stories could be told about pastors, church leaders and parents whose children abandoned their faith when they went to university. The Apostle Paul warned in Colossians 2:10 the danger of Christians being spoiled through listening to and taking in worldly philosophy. This is exactly what has happened to many of these young people. You can see the problem in America, in Britain it is probably worse!, Unless we as Christian parents prepare our young people to defend their Faith and answer the challenges they will face in university, we will lose them to the vain secular humanist philosophies of this world! (Colossians.2:8-10).

iii. We use apologetics in Evangelism because the Bible teaches us that all men can know God through Natural Revelation Romans 1:18-28[3]

Apologetics is defending the Christian Faith and refuting false beliefs and ideas that unbelievers hold onto. Often you will meet people who say that we cannot be sure whether there is a God or not because there is not enough proof or evidence. These are known as agnostics. Now the Bible clearly teaches us that God has given men ample evidence as to His existence in the things that are made (Romans 1:18-21). The Bible teaches that evidence for God's existence can be seen in the world and in the human heart and personality. This is known as Natural Revelation. What this means is that when we evangelise we are to use this Natural Revelation to persuade men and women that God exists (Romans 1:19-21)

Psalm 19:1-"The heavens declare the glory of God; and the firmament sheweth his handiwork."- creation points to God

Romans 1:20- "For the invisible things of him from the creation of the world are clearly seen, being understood by the things that are made "-man can see and know about God through the created order

Romans 2:14-15-"Which shew the work of the law written in their hearts, their conscience also bearing witness..." God's moral law is written on the hearts of all men and women.

Natural revelation shows men and women that there is a God. Special Revelation, the Bible, reveals His character ways to them, and how they can have a relationship with Him through Jesus Christ. When evangelising to people today, you will have to show them through nature that there is a God, before you can tell them who is He and the salvation He offers them in Christ.

iv. The Early Church defended the Faith and argued the truth of Christianity in their generation.[4]

Peter

- Acts 2:32, 3:15, 5:30-32, 10:39-40- he says he was an eyewitness to the resurrection and a witness to these things of the gospel he is preaching. He is bringing forth historical evidence for the Christian faith

Luke:
Luke 1:1-5, Acts 1:1Luke a doctor states clearly in his gospel that he faithfully recorded the facts down about the life, work and resurrection of the Lord Jesus Christ –He is presenting historical evidence to Theophilus, about the person and work of Jesus Christ

Paul
Acts 9:22-, 17:2, 17:31, 18:4, 19:8-10

The apostle Paul reasoned and disputed with the Jews and Gentiles about the truth of the person and work of Jesus Christ, in the synagogues, open air and in the school of the gentiles

E. Different Types of Apologetics[5]

"When the enemy comes in like a flood, the spirit of the Lord raises up a standard against him." Isaiah 59:9

We mentioned earlier that Apologetics is a form of spiritual warfare for the minds and hearts of men. Satan has endeavoured to bring every area of human knowledge under his influence. If we are to win people to Christ, we need to engage in many different forms of apologetics, and argue the case for Christ from different perspectives. Different types of apologetics deals with different areas where we can argue and persuade unbelievers that the Bible and the Christian Faith is truth itself. The following is a brief description of the different types and fields of apologetics that are being practised today.

1. *Philosophical Apologetics*- is concerned with answering basic questions about the nature of the world and the universe. One important question is whether God exists.

You will often meet people who deny the existence of God (atheists) or say God's existence cannot be proved (agnostics). This is what is happening today with the rise of the new atheism. Philosophical apologetics seeks to defend Christian belief through philosophical arguments for the existence of God. This can take the form of:

The ontological Argument-this argument states that if you were to think of God as the greatest being, for God to be that being He must exist in reality not just in your mind. Since God is the greatest being, you can think of, he must exist outside your mind, in actual reality. Therefore, he must exist; he must possess necessary existence to be the greatest being.

The Cosmological Argument-argument from the first cause - The first cause argument (or "cosmological argument") takes the existence of the universe to entail the existence of a being that created it. It does so based on the fact that the universe had a beginning. There must be a first cause to the beginning of the universe. . That first cause is God.

The argument from design, teleological argument - this argument infers from the intelligent order and created beauty of the universe that there is an intelligent Designer and Creator of the universe. If we see a painter, we know there must have been a painter. If we see a watch, we know that there had to be a watchmaker. From the intelligent way the universe is ordered, the laws of physics, chemistry and so on, we can infer that an intelligent mind created it. Order does not come out of Chaos. That intelligent mind is God

The Moral Argument - The moral argument appeals to the existence of moral laws as evidence of God's existence. According to this argument, there could not be such a thing as morality without God. Everyone knows that certain actions are intrinsically wrong. This proves that there is morality and moral law in the universe. The existence of a universal moral law means that there must be a supreme moral governor of the universe. This moral governor is God.

2. Historical Apologetics- deals with defending the credibility of the Bible, Old Testament and New Testament, their texts, and the historical occurrences they record. It includes defending the historical accuracy of recorded events in the Bible such as creation, the flood, and the person of Jesus Christ, that He actually existed, died and rose again, and the trustworthiness of the New Testament Gospels and Epistles. It also involves showing how the prophetic declarations of the Bible prove its divine authorship. The need for this type of apologetics was shown a number of years ago when Dan Brown wrote his book, The Da Vinci Code which went on to give an alternative account of the life of Jesus from the so called Gnostic Gospels. Even today, the real Gospels are being attacked as un-historical accounts of the life of Jesus.

3. Scientific Apologetics- presents scientific evidence for the truth of Christian faith. It uses information and data from Cosmology and biology to show that there had to be an intelligent creator behind the universe. Scientific apologetics argues that the only reasonable and rational explanation for the origin of the universe, the origin of life on Earth, the fine –tuning of the universe and the complexity of DNA is that there has to be an intelligent supernatural being that created and designed it all. This is the area being debated today in the evolution verses creation debates.

4. *Comparative religious apologetics*- defends the Christian Faith against the claims of other religions that teach that they and their teachings can lead man to God and Heaven. This form of apologetics argues for the uniqueness of Christ as the only religious teacher who died for the sins of mankind.

5. *Presuppositional Apologetics*-This is the defence of the Christian faith by arguing the absurdity of the other worldviews without God and showing their innate contradictions.

6. *Testimonial apologetics*- this form of apologetics uses personal testimony as evidence for the Christian faith. The apostle Paul used his testimony to defend the Christian faith to King Agrippa Acts 26:2- 24.

When you evangelise, you will find yourself involved in one of these types of apologetics. Understand that there are men who specialise in one of or all of these areas of apologetics and you will need to read up and research in these areas when you evangelise. If the person you witness to has objections to the Christian faith, find out what the objections are. Using the above list get the relevant information to answer their objections.

Chapter Two
Introduction to Atheistic Worldviews

In this chapter, we will briefly examine some worldviews that impact our society today. We cannot defend and argue for the Christian Faith if we do not know what we are up against. We will look at some of the worldviews that you will encounter when you begin to evangelise people in your town or city. These can be divided into two groups, Atheistic Worldviews - those that do not believe in a God, and Theistic worldviews - those who believe in God such as Islam and Christian sects such as Jehovah Witnesses.

What is Worldview?

"For as he thinketh in his heart, so is he..." Proverbs 27:3

The word "worldview" is made up of two words, world, which means world as we know it and view, meaning opinion, persuasion. A worldview is simply the way a person sees and perceives the world; it is their outlook on life. It is how a person interprets and sees the world. A worldview gives a person an explanation about the world and universe and how the facts of reality relate and fit together. There are as many worldviews as there are people. All religions, philosophies and ideologies are worldviews, a set of ideas that interpret the world in a certain way. For instance, a Hindu worldview would see human life as being enslaved to the cycle of rebirth, Karma, where a person is constantly reborn into another form of life until they are purified and escape the cycle of rebirth. A Naturalistic worldview sees human beings as material physical beings with no soul or spirit, no god(s) or afterlife.

We mentioned above that worldviews are either atheistic or theistic. It is important for us to understand how to evangelise these different groups of people. What is our aim when we evangelise people with an atheistic worldview? What is our aim when we evangelise people with a theistic worldview? The rule is as follows:

(a)   When we evangelise people with atheistic worldviews, we are initially trying to persuade and GET THEM TO SEE THE TRUTH THAT THERE IS A GOD. Once we get them to acknowledge this then we can preach the Gospel to them.

(b)   When we evangelise people with theistic worldviews, we are trying to get them to see that THEY CANNOT ATTAIN HEAVEN OR ACCEPTANCE WITH GOD THROUGH THEIR OWN WORKS/EFFORTS. Once we get them to acknowledge this then we can preach Christ to them as the only person able to get them to Heaven (John 14:6).

Question

What is a worldview?

_____

Atheistic Worldviews

There are many forms of non-theistic worldviews we could look at, such as Marxism, Naturalism, Scepticism, Freudianism, Existentialism, Secular Humanism and Evolution. In this course, we will look at Secular Humanism, Evolution and the New Atheism.

1. Secular Humanism

Secular Humanism is a non-theistic philosophy that promotes man as the measure of all things. The word "secular" means this world, this age, this temporal sphere excluding the religious and divine. The word "Humanism" is the belief in mankind as the measure of all things. Secular Humanism is the philosophy that is concerned with man and his present temporal world and rejects God and all supernatural beliefs. It centres itself on humanity and the improvement of life in this world. Its roots can be traced back to the ancient Greeks particularly Protagoras whose slogan "man the Measure" has become the humanistic basic creed. Secular Humanism has become the philosophy of the Western nations, influencing society, politics and culture. It is a philosophy that rejects all supernatural and religious dogmas as the basis of morality, education and social policy and replaces it with human reason, justice and ethics. Secular Humanism believes that human beings can lead good, happy and fruitful lives without the help of gods and supernatural beliefs. Secular humanists are atheists and naturalists. They reject the supernatural and believe that the universe is a closed physical system. Since there is no god(s) there can be no absolute standards of right and wrong behaviour; all is relative dependent upon the circumstances and situation a person finds themselves in. Secular Humanists argue that since "man is the measure of all things" mankind not God or religious beliefs are the basis of truth and values.

Modern Secular Humanism has been influenced by the ideas of the Enlightenment thinkers of the seventeenth and eighteenth centuries. Atheists, sceptics, deists and agnostics such as Denis Diderot (1713–1784), Baron D'Holbach (1723–1789) François Voltaire (1694-1778), Emmanuel Kant (1724-1804), Thomas Paine (1737-1809), and Jean-Jacques Rousseau (1712-1778) stressed human reasoning over faith in the Bible and obedience to the Church. These thinkers taught that humanity should divorce itself from God and religion, and should create its own values and political ideas. Man is part of nature that is a biological machine. These views helped shaped Western culture and civilisation. Some of these ideas were the basis of the first and second Humanist manifestos of 1933 and 1973. Secular Humanism has become the predominant philosophy in Western nations simply because these nations separated religion from government. In the absence of a religious belief system to guide public policies, Secular Humanism has filled in the void left by religion to become the philosophy that influences all political, moral and social legislation. The British Humanist Association launched the Atheist bus Campaign in 2009, trying to influence people with their atheism and humanism. Some famous humanists include Barack Obama Senior, Albert Einstein, Brad Pitt, Carl Sagan, Gene Rodenberry – creator of Star Trek, and Paul Kurtz founder of the Council for Secular Humanism in the United States.

What Secular Humanists Believe and their objections against Religion

The British Association of Humanists say that "they......are atheists and agnostics who make sense of the world using reason, experience and shared human values. We take responsibility for our actions and base our ethics on the goals of human welfare, happiness and fulfilment. We seek to make the best of the one life we have by creating meaning and purpose for ourselves, individually and together."[6]

Humanists deny the existence of God and the supernatural – "We find insufficient evidence for belief in the existence of a supernatural; it is either meaningless or irrelevant to the question of survival and fulfilment of the human race" Humanist Manifesto II 1973

Humanists see religion and religious belief as harmful to humanity – "We believe, however, that traditional dogmatic or authoritarian religions that place revelation, God, ritual, or creed above human needs and experience do a disservice to the human species. Any account of nature should pass the tests of scientific evidence; in our judgment, the dogmas and myths of traditional religions do not do so...Promises of immortal salvation or fear of eternal damnation are both illusory and harmful. They distract humans from present concerns, from self-actualization, and from rectifying social injustices." Humanist Manifesto II 1973

Humanists view the world and the universe as a closed physical system – Humanists see man as essentially good and not sinful as opposed to the Biblical view (Romans 3:23): "Man is at last becoming aware that he alone is responsible for the realization of the world of his dreams, that he has within himself the power for its achievement. He must set intelligence and will to the task." Humanist Manifest 1, 1933

Humanists see salvation and deliverance for humanity in science and reason, not in an external supernatural saviour: "Reason and intelligence are the most effective instruments that humankind possesses. There is no substitute: neither faith nor passion suffices in itself. The controlled use of scientific methods, which have transformed the natural and social sciences since the Renaissance, must be extended further in the solution of human problems." Humanist Manifesto II 1973

Morality and Ethics do not come from God or a holy book but from human experience and life, there are no absolute rights and wrongs: "We affirm that moral values derive their source from human experience. Ethics is autonomous and situational needing no theological or ideological sanction. Ethics stems from human need and interest." Humanist Manifesto II, 1973

Secular Humanism is the philosophy that is challenging Christianity and all religions today. It is successful because it appeals to all men and women since it is based in human needs and wants. It is shaping social policy on marriage, family, sexuality, abortion, euthanasia, assisted suicide, stem cell research and many other issues.

HOW TO RESPOND TO SECULAR HUMANISTS

We will be looking in more detail in Chapter four at how to respond to all these worldviews. Here are some general objections that can be made against Secular Humanism, that clearly show it is false.

i. The inherent flawed nature of humans beings. The secular humanist belief in the goodness of man and the human personality is grossly mistaken. Man is not good nor can achieve his own salvation. Evidence for this is shown in the two devastating world wars, and the continual wars going on today. Crime, rape, robbery, gun crime continue and are getting worse in some places. Starvation, pollution and extinction of animal species are happening because of man's misuse of the planet's resources. The breakdown of families and relationships, all point to man's inherent flawed nature. Only the Christian doctrine of salvation offers an intelligent and meaningful response to man's inherent flawed nature and this deliverance was provided in the person and work of Jesus Christ.

ii.   Science and technological progress has not "saved" humanity.

Science and technology although they have helped humanity can hardly be said to be its salvation. The ecological damage to the planet, the Ozone layer, seas, rain forests, animal kingdom is all the result of scientific and technological progress. This "technological progress" now threatens the very survival of the human race on the planet Earth. The truth is that science without God becomes another destructive force in the hands of fallen, human beings.

Questions

What is secular Humanism?
_____

List two objections Secular humanists have against the Christian Faith
_____
_____
_____

2. Evolution-Naturalism

"It is often supposed that when people stop believing in God, they believe in nothing. Alas, it is worse than that. When they stop believing in God, they believe in anything." G. K. Chesterton

Evolution is the theory that claims to explain the origins of human life on Earth without the need for a divine creator. Charles Darwin the English Botanist 1809-1882 was the man who popularised the theory of Evolution. In 1859, he published his book "Origin of Species" which explained his theory of how life originated on planet Earth. Darwin said that life on Earth began millions of years ago when small living cells evolved and developed into higher animals and species we see today. The mechanism for this change he called Natural Selection, a process of nature whereby weaker animals were weeded out and the stronger of the species survived passing their Genes onto the next generation: "In the struggle for survival, the fittest win out at the expense of their rivals because they succeed in adapting themselves best to their environment." (Charles Darwin). The process of Natural selection triggers changes and adaptations within an animal species causing them to adapt to their environments(s). These changes and modifications of animals Darwin argued even caused them to evolve into a totally new animal species (Evolution). Before the publication of Darwin's book, most of the world believed in God and the Genesis account of creation. Darwin's book changed forever how men saw themselves, God and the Universe.

Evolution commonly referred to as naturalistic evolution accounts for man, and all forms of life on Earth without the need for a creator. Life started on Earth "spontaneously" when simple complex chemicals came together to form life. All that was need was a combination of atoms, movement, time and chance. These simple life forms began to evolve and change. Their sole purpose was to survive and reproduce. This is their only purpose according to Darwinian evolution. These life forms began to make slight mutations or changes in their genetic make-up enabling them to adapt to their environment and reproduce offspring. Today we see different animals and creatures that over millions of years successfully made the genetic changes which resulted in physical changes that enabled them to adapt to their environments and reproduce. *Human beings are a result of these slight genetic changes in the ape family, the primates over millions of years that produced modern man.* This view of human origins has become the standard scientific model in the Western Word. It is taught throughout schools and universities and has replaced the Biblical account of creation. Today its foremost supporter is the neo- Darwinist Richard Dawkins. Dawkins recently published a book entitled "The Greatest Show on Earth" in which he presented the so-called "evidence" for evolution and argued that it was a scientific fact. Today there are debates between evolutionists and Bible believing Christians- Creationists. The New Atheists strongly promote Evolution and are on a campaign to rid the world of Biblical Creationism which they see as false. There are Christian organisations who present the Biblical view of creation such as Answers in Genesis, the Discovery Institute and other Creationist organisations. These organisations refute evolution from a scientific perspective. Of note is the Intelligent Design Movement. The Intelligent Design movement argues that certain features of the universe and of living things are best explained by an intelligent cause, not an undirected process such as natural selection. Evolution although unproved has become the "secular gospel" of the modern era. Charles Darwin the promoter of the theory once said: "My work is the devil's gospel" (*Life and Letters*, Vol. 2, p. 124.)

What Evolutionists Believe and their objections against Religion

Evolutionists have similar objections as secular humanists against God and the bible. Some of them include the following:

Evolution, *not God, is responsible for the origin of life on Earth.*

Evolution argues that life originated from inanimate matter - "abiogenesis".

Science can explain the world without reference to God so God does not exist: "I am aware that the assumed instinctive belief in God has been used by many persons as an argument for his existence. The idea of a universal and beneficent Creator does not seem to arise in the mind of man, until he has been exposed to culture." (Charles Darwin, Descent of Man p. 612).

The Earth is billions of years old as opposed to the 6,000 years recorded in the Bible. *Carbon 14 dating can prove that the Earth is millions of years old.*

Mankind was not made by God but evolved from lower forms of life – man is an animal not a superior being: "We can allow satellites, planets, suns, universe, nay whole systems of universes to be governed by laws, but the smallest insect, we wish to be created at once by special act." (Charles Darwin)

The Fossil Record *proves that life on Earth evolved and was not the result of special divine creation. Man evolved from lower life forms.*

Natural selection not Divine Providence *is the force that governs and determines life on Earth including human life.*

Science gives us the answer to all the problems *and difficulties of life not a holy book such as the Bible.*

Questions:

What does the theory of evolution say about the origin of life on Earth?

List two objections evolutionists have against the Christian Faith

_____

_____

HOW TO RESPOND TO EVOLUTIONISTS

In chapter four of this book, we look in more detail in how to respond to the objections of evolutionists against Christianity. I will just list two powerful objections to the theory of Evolution.

i. The Origin of life cannot be explained by the theory of Evolution. Evolutionists cannot explain or prove that life originated from inanimate matter – "abiogenesis". Stanley Miller's experiment of 1958 in which he attempted to create life in a laboratory, failed. Dr. Stanley Miller and Dr. Sidney Fox were two of the first scientists to attempt laboratory experiments aimed at trying to prove that life could arise spontaneously. They designed a Pyrex apparatus containing methane, ammonia, and water vapour, but no oxygen. Through this mixture, they passed electric sparks to simulate lightning strikes. Result no life was produced, although the electricity did combine some atoms to form amino acids the building blocks of life. Although at the time this experiment was hailed as a success, because of the presence of amino acids, scientists now know that the conditions of the Earth were different from what Miller assumed when he done his experiments. In other words, the early conditions of the Earth would have made it impossible to produce these amino acids, which are the building blocks of life. To this day no one has created life or knows how to go about creating it from inanimate matter. All the claims of producing life that we hear about is simply man using existing life forms and modifying them in some way. He starts off with life and modifies life, but cannot create life! This is a huge blow to the theory of evolution because if you cannot explain how life began, how can you assume to explain how life has evolved?

ii. The Lack of Transitional forms in the Fossil Record.

There are no transitional fossils that conclusively prove evolution occurred in animals or man. Darwin himself admitted "The number of intermediate varieties which formerly existed on Earth should be truly enormous. Why then is not every geological formation and every stratum full of such intermediate links? Geology assuredly does not reveal any such graduated organic chain. *and this perhaps is the most obvious and gravest objection to my theory.*" Do we find 150 years later any fossils that conclusively prove evolution? No, nothing much has changed since Darwin wrote his book. The evolutionist Steven Gould once said about the fossil record, "the extreme rarity of transitional forms in the fossil record remains as the trade secret of palaeontology." Evolutionists have tried to fudge information and claim that a fossil such as the Archaeopteryx is a transitional species between reptiles and birds. Colin Patterson FRS who was once responsible for the fossilized remains of Archaeopteryx in the Natural History Museum said of the fossil record: " I will lay it on the line- there is not one fossil (a fossil that is ancestral or transitional) for which one could make a watertight case." Note these are famous evolutionists who admit that the fossil evidence does not support the theory of Evolution!

3. The New Atheism

Atheism is the belief that there is no God. Atheism is not new it has been around for centuries. All Marxists, secular humanists and Freudians are Atheists. Since the 2011 census in the United Kingdom, 14.1 million people said that they had no religion accounting for 25% of the population. Atheism is on the rise. There is even an atheist Church in Britain! This is due to a rise of a new form of militant atheism that has a political and social agenda. It aims to expose what it sees as the delusional nature of religion and rid it from society. This Atheism arose in part as a result of the 9-11 terrorist attacks in New York. Sam Harris wrote a book entitled the *The End of Faith: Religion, Terror, and the Future of Reason* (2004). He began to write this book the day after the attacks on America, in September 2001. In it, he argues that the values and principles of the Enlightenment were under threat by religious fanaticism. Richard Dawkins wrote his infamous book "The God Delusion" in 2006, which has sold over two million copies to date. Daniel Dennett wrote his book" Breaking the Spell – Religion as a Natural Phenomenon" and Christopher Hitchens wrote his book "God is Not Great – How religion poisons Everything." These four men are the leaders of a New Atheism which is having a considerable impact today especially amongst young people and college students. Richard Dawkins wrote "The God Delusion" with the express purpose of converting religious people to atheism. In it he says that he hopes that "religious readers who open it will be atheists when they put it down." This has certainly happened to many Christians and Muslims who have become atheists. The New Atheism seeks to educate and warn the world of the dangers of religion and to replace it with reason and science as the new guardians of society.

The area it has taken up its attack against religion is in the field of science and biological evolution. Dawkins regularly attacks and debates Christians on the questions of the origin of life and the nature of religion. The New Atheists fiercely attack the Christian doctrine of creation and attempt to prove how science and evolution have shown to Bible to be false. The New Atheism sees religious faith as ignorance and a blind refusal to accept the scientific facts of Evolution. The New Atheists see themselves on a crusade to save the world from the terrors and dangers of religion and religious people. They carry out their crusade through education and social action. They use education to convert people to their views. Dawkins, Dennett, Hitchens and Harris regularly conduct live media debates with Christians, on University campuses, radio, and produce TV programmes to bring their message across to the world.

The New Atheist objections to God and religion are similar to those of the humanists and evolutionists:

There is no God and the universe *is the type of universe you would expect it to be if there were no God:* Richard Dawkins has said in his book river out of Eden, the the Universe has the characteristics we would expect it to have if there were no purpose, God or design in it.

Religious believers are delusional, *believing in something that is not true – faith believes things that are untrue:* Sam Harris has said in His book Letter to a Christian nation it is time to admit that faith is simply an excuse religious people use to believe things we all know to be untrue.

Religion and beliefs are bad for society. Religion breeds intolerance, hatred and violence as seen in the terrorist acts of 9/11.

Religion teaches people to suspend *their mind and intellect and believe in myths* Dawkins opposes religion because he believes it teaches people to be content in not understanding of how the world really works.

Religious beliefs are memes, *mind viruses passed on from one generation to the next. A mind virus- a meme causes religion.*

Science and rational investigation are the only truth and hold out the hope for humanity's future: Christopher Hitchens said that now we have scientific instruments such as the telescope and microscope, religion no longer can offer explanations about the world we live in.

Religious indoctrination of *children is form of mental child abuse and should be stopped*: 'What shall we tell the children?' is an argument presented by the Psychologist Nicholas Humprey that since religious indoctrination of children is a form if child abuse, we should work to free children from religions which damage their minds. Richard Dawkins agrees with this and argues that religious indoctrination is child abuse.

Religion should be viewed and **investigated** *as any other natural natural phenomenon;* how it evolved its purpose and its future.

Atheists agnostics and sceptics should challenge religion and attempt to convert society to sane reasoning – science and atheism.

HOW TO RESPOND TO THE NEW ATHEISTS

The New Atheism cannot account for universal laws that it uses which lie outside the physical realm of our existence.

i. If man is a product of blind, indifferent evolution then where do the laws of logic, mathematics and reason come from which lie outside the material realm of man's physical existence? Why do atheists trust and rely upon these laws if their very brains are the product of chance accidental processes? The laws of logic, reason and mathematics, point to a higher dimension of human existence and of the Universe- a spiritual, supernatural mind where these laws originate.

The New Atheism claims that religious belief is a leap in the dark is erroneous.

ii. Faith and particularly the Christian Faith is not a blind leap in the dark, but is based on scientific, rational evidence. Evidence for the existence of the person of Jesus Christ, evidence that the universe with its laws and principles point to an intelligent mind behind it. Many prominent scientists are theists and have concluded that the only rational, intelligent explanation of how the universe came into being is the Christian account as recorded in the book of Genesis.

Questions

What is the New Atheism?

_____

List two objections the new atheists have against religious belief

_____

_____

List down 2 books the new atheists have written

_____

_____

List down 2 argument against the New Atheism

_____

_____

Chapter Three

Introduction to Theistic Worldviews

In this chapter, we will look at two religious worldviews, Islam and Jehovah Witnesses. Islam is a major world religion, while Jehovah witnesses is a sect or cult, a deviation of true Christianity. Religious belief systems are man's attempt to reach God and Heaven by his own works, his own effort. It does not matter what the religion is and what its beliefs are, it is ultimately rooted in man striving to be good by following a set of rules or laws. It is important when we evangelise religious people that we remember the following important points:

i.   Our aim when we evangelise them is to try to persuade them by using their own beliefs and their consciences that they will never be good enough to get to Heaven or please God by their own works.

ii. Each religion we encounter has a ruling principality in the heavenly places that is influencing the hearts and minds of men and women (Ephesians 6:10-12). When we go out to evangelise an area, we must first engage in spiritual warfare over the area and bind the religious powers controlling the hearts and minds of the people in the area (Matthew 18:19-20, 1 Corinthians 15:32, 2 Corinthians 4:4, Ephesians 6:10-12).

Islam

Definition of Islam

Islam is the second major world religion today with an estimated 1.5 billion followers worldwide. Islam literally means submission, submission to Allah. Those who practice Islam are known as Muslims. A Muslim is a person who submits to the will of God. The prophet Muhammad who lived around the 7th Century AD founded

Islam. Islam has many beliefs that are similar to Judaism and Christianity. In fact, Muslims regard certain parts of the Bible as the word of God. They believe that God spoke through some of the prophets of the Bible and view Jesus as a great prophet. However, they believe that the last prophet God sent to the Earth, who is a continuation of the Old Testament prophets, was the prophet Muhammad. Muslims believe that Muhammad was visited by the angel Gabriel and received a series of revelations in a cave that he was told to write down, and which later became the Qur'an, the Holy book of Islam. Muslims believe that it is through prayer, good works and following the teachings of the Qur'an and Hadith that a person attains Paradise. Islam has three major groups; the Sunni, the sh'ites and the Sufis. The majority of Muslims are Sunnis. The Sunnis believe that they are the real Muslims, followers of the prophet.

Mohammed

The prophet Muhammad is the founder of Islam. He lived in Mecca around 570 AD. Both of his parents died in his infancy so his grandfather raised him then by his uncle. He was born into the Quraysh tribe. When his grandfather died he was raised by his uncle Abu talib. He began to work for a wealthy widow when he was 25, khadijah who was so impressed by his work that she proposed marriage. He married her and they had six children, two boys who died in infancy and four girls. When khadijah eventually died, he married several times, and had about 12 wives and three concubines.

It was in A.D.610 that he began to have visitations from the angel Gabriel, which he was told to write down. These revelations eventually became the Quran, the holy book of Islam. In 610 A.D, he had a visitation from the angel Gabriel in a dream who gave him the revelations that became the teachings of the Qur'an. Muhammad shared these visions with his wife Khadijah who along with his cousin Ali and a friend Au Bakr, became his first followers. He first began to preach his revelations to his family, but people in Mecca began to hear about his message and many became Muslims. It is claimed that God then began to command him to preach the message to all men, which he began to do in Mecca.

However because Mecca was an idolatrous city, when he began to preach against its idols he got persecuted. Because of this in the year 622 A.D., Muhammad fled o medina MEDINA- the city of the prophet. This significant event is called the Hijra and marks the first year of the Muslim calendar. In medina, he gathered a large following and began to attack caravans and those who opposed him in medina. Through a series raids and attacks against various groups, Arabs, Jews and certain towns, he eventually subdued medina and formed an umma, a theocracy under his control. With medina as his base, he led raids on other towns and eventually conquered Mecca in 630 A.D. It is true to say that the spread of Islam was just as much by the sword as it was by the preached word. Muhammad had many sayings and teachings which Muslims regard as authoritative. The sayings and teachings of Muhammad are called the Hadith. Muhammad died in Medina in 631 A.D. aged 61.

Questions:

What does the word Islam mean?

_____

_____

How did Muhammad receive his revelations?

_____

Who were Muhammad's first followers/disciples?

How and where did Muhammad establish the first Muslim community?

Doctrines of Islam: What Muslims Believe.

The Five central beliefs of the Islamic faith (Iman)

1. In One God- they deny the Trinity of God:

"Know, therefore, that there is no god but Allah, and ask forgiveness for your fault..." (Sura 47: 19)

"In the name of God, the Merciful, the Compassionate. Say (O Muhammad) He is God the One God, the Everlasting Refuge, who has not begotten, nor has been begotten and equal to Him is not anyone."

The Qu'ran teaches that Allah is Lord of Heaven and Earth, creator and sustainer of all things, and all powerful who will judge all men at the final judgement. Muslims have ninety nine names for God that they recite regularly in prayer. Muhammed in the Hadith, said that he who memorised these names would go to Paradise. Muslims flatly deny the trinity and teach that any one who believes in the doctrine of the trinity commits an unforgivable sin. To say that there are three persons in Godhead is to commit the sin of idolatry-an unforgivable sin-"shirk"-the sin of associating a creature with the deity

2. **Angels – the messenger angel they believe to be Gabriel, brought Allah's word to the prophet Mohammed.**

"Whoever is an enemy to Gabriel – the one who has brought the Qur'an down upon your heart, [O Muhammad], by the will of Allah, confirming that which was before it and as guidance and good tidings for the believers." (Sura 2:97-98

"The Messenger believes in what has been revealed to him from his Lord, and so do the believers. All believe in Allah, His Angels and His Messengers." (Sura 2:285)

Muslims believe in angels both good and bad. Angels are important as they carry the revelations of God to man. It was the angel Gabriel that revealed Allah's revelation to Mohammed, so they are important bearers of God's Will and commandments. Muslims believe that there are in four archangels: Gabriel (the angel of revelation), Michael (the angel of providence), Israfil (the angel of doom), and Izra'il (the angel of death). Ministering angels include recording angels, throne-bearers, and questioners of the dead. There are also fallen angels whose chief is Iblis, or Shaytan. Muslims believe in another group of supernatural beings called the Jinn, who are created from fire and can be good or bad. They were created by Allah to worship God along with the rest of humankind (Sura 51:56).

3. **Holy Books recognised in Islam include, parts of the Old Testament, the Gospel and the Qu'ran and Hadith.**

"We believe in Allah, and in what has been revealed to us and what was revealed to Abraham, Ishmail, Isaac, Jacob, and the Tribes, and in (the Books) given to Moses, Jesus, and the Prophets, from their Lord: We make no distinction between one and another among them ." (Sura 3:84).

"Those who follow the Messenger (Mohammed), the Prophet who can neither read nor write, whom they will find described in the Torah and the Gospel (which are) with them (Sura 7:157).

Islam teaches that the Torah of Moses, the Psalms of David, the Injil (Gospel) of Jesus, and the Quran, are revelations from Allah to mankind. However, Muslims believe that last and final Testament of God to mankind was the Qur'an delivered to Muhammad. Although Muslims talk about the Torah, Psalms, and Gospels, they do not mean the same Old and New Testaments that Christians have in their Bibles. They believe that the original Torah, Psalms, and Gospel have been corrupted and lost. What Christians have in the Old and New Testaments are not God's Word or revelation. The Qu'ran they regard as the last Testament and revelation of God to man and so has final authority even over the Bible. The Qu'ran is the Holy book of Islam, Muslims revere this book and they believe that it has not been corrupted since the time it was written down. The Quran literally means "recitation", as Muhammed recited it as it was given to him from the angel Gabriel. The Qu'ran is roughly four fifths the size of the New Testament. It consists of 116 suras (chapters) each with a different topic heading. Muslims also hold the sayings and acts of the prophet Muhammed as authorative for guidance and living. These are called the Hadith and are revered in Islam and come second only to the Qur'an.

4. Prophets

"Believe in all that was revealed to Abraham, Ishmael, Isaac, Jacob, and the tribes, and that which Moses and Jesus received (2:136*).

Muslims believe that God sent prophets to mankind to warn them and teach them his ways. The Quran mentions twenty five by name. Some of these include Adam, Noah, Abraham, Moses, Isaac, Jacob, Ishmael, Joseph, David, Solomon, Elijah, Elisha, and Jonah from Old Testament times. There are others from New Testament times, John the Baptist, and Jesus. The Quran affirms the Virgin

Birth of Jesus (although not His eternal pre-existence), but teaches that the Crucifixion and Resurrection did not happen as recorded in the Gospels. The Quran includes some of the miracles and moral teachings of Jesus but does not mention His lordship or His divinity. Although Islam recognises Jesus to be a great prophet, it does not see him as God or the son of God:

"People of the Book, go not beyond the bounds in your religion, and say not as to God but the truth. The Messiah, Jesus son of Mary, was only the Messenger of God, and His Word that He committed to Mary, and a Spirit from Him. So believe in God and His Messengers, and say not, 'Three.' Refrain; better is it for you. God is only one God. Glory be to Him - (He is) above having a son." (4:171)

Muhammad is considered the last and the greatest of the prophets. He is the "Seal of the Prophets", after who no more will come. Muslims believe that he was "prepared for and attested to by all the preceding prophets." The Muslims consider Islam as the oldest monotheistic religion in the world.

5. The Day of Judgement

"Verily the day of sorting out is a thing appointed, the day that the trumpet shall be sounded, and ye shall come forth in crowds; and the heavens shall be opened as if there were doors, and the mountains shall vanish, as if they were a mirage. Truly hell is as a place of ambush, for the transgressors a place of destination: They will dwell therein for ages." (Sura 17:17-18)

"Surely the dwellers of the garden shall on that day be in a place quite happy. They and their wives shall be in shaded, reclining on raised couches. They shall have fruits therin, and they shall have whatsoever they desire." (Sura 36:55-57).

Judgment Day in Islamic theology will be preceded by signs, then announced by a trumpet blast (Sura 17:17-18, Sura 36:55-57). The dead will arise bodily from their graves and join the living, and then all will be examined one by one and assigned to Paradise or Hell. No one can escape this judgment. The Qu'ran gives vivid pictures of the balance scales that will be used to weigh the good and evil deeds of each soul, even to the weight of a mustard seed. Pious believers in Allah can expect abundant sensual pleasures in Paradise. There will be perpetual luxury, physical comfort, food, clear water, mansions, servants, lovely maidens, and virgins. The wicked will suffer and swelter in the hot blasts, foul smoke, and molten metal of Hell, whilst the righteous shall experience the rewards of paradise.

Questions:

List down the five essential beliefs of Islam and describe what they mean for a Muslims

_____

_____

_____

_____

Islamic Religious Practices: The Five Pillars of Islam

Islam is built upon certain practices that all Muslims must obey. They are called the five Pillars of Islam. If followed faithfully they will lead a person into paradise. The five pillars are:

i. **Shahada** - The reciting of their statement of faith about God and Mohammed.

The first of the Five Pillars of Islam is the **shahada**. *Shahada* is the Muslim profession of faith, expressing the two key beliefs that make one a Muslim:

La ilaha illa Allah wa-Muhammad rasul Allah.

"There is no god but Allah and Muhammad is the prophet of God."

Islam teaches that sincere recitation of this confession of faith before two Muslims is the only condition to make a person become a Muslim and become involved in the Muslim community. It represents acceptance not only of Allah and his prophet, but of the entirety of Islam. The *shahada* must be recited correctly aloud with full understanding and with the hart once in every Muslim's lifetime. It is from this basic belief that the other doctrines of Islam are developed.

ii. **Salat** - ritual prayer which has to be done five times a day – head bowing towards Mecca. Muslims to pray five times a day the average time being five to ten minutes. Prayer times are dawn, afternoon, late afternoon, after sunset, and at night.

Prayer is always directed in the direction (*qibla*) of the Ka'ba shrine in Mecca. A prayer mat, *sajjada*, is commonly used during prayer times. Prayer may be performed individually, but is more advantageous to the individual if done with other Muslims. The focal prayer of the week is the midday prayer at the mosque on Fridays. *Salat* must always be preceded by ablutions (*wudu'*) of ritually washing the face, hands, and feet. This can be done with sand when water is not available. (Qur'an, Suras: 2:222, 4:43, 5:6

iii. ***Zakat***- this is a charity tax, where Muslims give 2.5% of their income to the poor. This is to be done privately; however, there are many Muslims organisations that encourage Muslims to give Zakat to areas in the world where there is a need.

iv. Sawm - fasting-Muslims fast in the month of Ramadan for 40 days during this time they abstain from food, liquor and sexual relations. Muslims are allowed to eat and drink at sunset and some Muslims will get up before sunrise to eat before the start of the fast.

v. ***Hajj*** – this is the pilgrimage to Mecca, the Holy City for Muslims. Muslims are required once in their lifetime to make this pilgrimage to Mecca. Whilst on the pilgrimage, they will visit Muslim holy sites, such as the Ka'aba and the city of Medina.

Questions:

List down the five pillars of Islam

_____

_____

_____

_____

_____

What Muslims Believe and their objections against Christianity

"The Bible of the Christians and Jews has been corrupted, *and this is why Allah revealed the Qu'ran to Mohammad'.*

Muslims attack the Christian doctrine of the trinity *saying that we believe in three gods.*

Muslims deny that Jesus is God or the son of God *saying it is impossible for God to have a son as this would mean he had relations with a woman.*

Jesus was not crucified *it only appeared so they will quote the Qu'ran Sura 4:547.*

Muslims object to the Christian doctrine of salvation through Jesus Christ. *On the Day to Judgement, a person will be fairly judged according to his faith, his actions, and his efforts to sincerely repent.*

Ultimately, however, it is the Mercy and Forgiveness of God *that will admit a person to Paradise, and not just his faith and deeds.*

HOW TO RESPOND TO MUSLIMS

Muslims tend to be extremely passionate and emotional about their faith, so you need to be very wise and careful when you defend your faith to them, especially the deity of Christ. Here are some guidelines that would be helpful when you enter into a debate with Muslims.

Do not offend the prophet Mohammed or the Qu'ran – Muslims revere these highly. You also need to understand the seriousness of religion for a Muslim. For them to convert to Christianity would be considered apostasy and punishable by death. In witnessing to a Muslim, you must be aware that the person you are speaking to, if they accept Christ, will probably be persecuted and could even be killed. It is important therefore that you know a place where they could find refuge, care, support and protection from other Muslims.

For a Muslim his family and community provides each member with their health insurance, their job, their food, their fellowship, their mate, and practically everything else of importance in life. When we win a Muslim to Christianity then we need to be prepared to make the necessary sacrifice and disciple them. They need much more of our time and love because we have torn them from their support system and we must find a way to support them.

A typical Muslim will know more about Christianity than a Christian will know about Islam. Just as Christians are taught how to witness to others, many Muslims are being taught how to refute the Christians' arguments thus making our witness ineffective. We need to know what Muslims believe in order to be able to refute them!

i) Some Muslims argue that the Bible has been corrupted by Christians and so cannot be relied upon. However, point out to Muslims that the Qu'ran does not say anything of the sort, but sees the Bible as the Word of God.

"He sent down to you this scripture, truthfully, confirming all previous scriptures, and He sent down the Torah and the Gospel". Sura. 3.3.

"And in their footsteps (of Moses and the Jews). We sent Jesus the son of Mary, attesting to (the truth of) the Torah which was between his hands; and we gave him the Gospel – therein is guidance and light and attesting to (the truth of) the Torah which was between his hands: a guidance and an admonition to the righteous." (Sura 5:19)

Other references in the Qu'ran that confirm this include: Surah 2:41, 89, 91, 97, 101, Surah 3:3, 50, 81, Surah 35:31, Surah 46:12, 30, Surah 61:6)

Show them that if their own holy book says and confirms the Torah, Psalms and Gospel who are they to say otherwise? Also, the Bible could not have been changed after Mohammed because we have the Hebrew and Greek manuscripts from which our present Bibles have been written. These have not changed and can be checked. After you have explained this to a Muslim, then challenge them if they have lived according to the Torah, Psalms, Gospel and Qu'ran to bring them to a place of Conviction of Sin.

ii)   Jesus did not die on the cross:

"And their saying, "We have killed the Messiah, Jesus, the son of Mary, the messenger of Allah." And they did not kill him, nor did they crucify him; but another was made to resemble him to them." Sura 4:156

Explain to the Muslim that you understand their concern that it is ignoble for a holy prophet to die in such a way. However, the truth is that He did die on the cross. Mohammed's account in the Qu'ran is 600 years after the event, and he lived miles away from Bethlehem. The prophets speak clearly of the death of Christ in Psalms 22, Isaiah 53:1-9 as do the Gospels. Muslims believe the Gospels are from God and they are four accounts of the Crucifixion event. Not only that there are other authors outside the Christian Faith who record Christ's death.

i.   Mara Bar-Serapio, a Stoic philosopher from ancient Syria, refers in his letter to the Jews executing their wise king

ii.   The Roman historian Tacitus mentions that "Christus...suffered the extreme penalty during the reign of Tiberius at the hands of one of our procurators..."*(Annals)*

iii. Also, Josephus, a first century Jewish historian, who wrote *The Antiquities of the Jews,* says the following:

"He [Christ] won over to Him many Jews and Gentiles and when Pilate at the suggestion of the principle men among us had condemned Him to the cross, those who had loved Him first did not forsake Him." *Antiquities of the Jews*

Explain to the Muslim that there is too much evidence even from outside Christianity to the fact that Jesus died on the Cross of Calvary, therefore the account in the Qu'ran cannot be accurate.

Question

List down two responses we can give to Muslim objectives against Christianity

_____

_____

_____

_____

Jehovah Witnesses

Basic Facts about Jehovah Witnesses

Jehovah Witnesses are a cult that denies the Trinity, the deity of Christ and the deity of the Holy Spirit. They are a millennial sect founded in 1870 in Pennsylvania by Charles Taize Russell. Their goal is to establish God's Kingdom, which they believe, will follow the Last battle, Armageddon. They are also known as Russellties. They number around 7.9 million people worldwide.

Founder of the Jehovah Witnesses Charles Taize Russell: 1852-1916

Like most of those who start sects and cults, Charles Russell was once a Christian Presbyterian and Congregationalist. Was born on 16th February 1852, in Pittsburgh Pennsylvania. His mother died when he was young and he developed a close relationship with his father. He was brought up as a Christian, a Congregationalist. He was evangelistic in his youth, but developed doubts about Christianity and dabbled for a while with Eastern religions. He became disillusioned with religion but after hearing a preacher by the name of Wendall, he came back to Christianity and began to study the Bible for himself.

After his own study of the Bible that he claimed was unbiased, Russell began to teach that many of the doctrines of Christianity were not biblical. He began to reject many of its doctrines and taught others to do the same. Russell and his group denied the doctrines of the Trinity and the divinity of Jesus Christ, the soul of man and eternal Hell. Being influenced by Adventist beliefs about the second imminent return of Christ, he taught that Christ was soon to return and men must be ready for his return. Russell soon got together people who listened to his views and started his own Bible studies. He adopted Adventist beliefs about the return of Christ but soon changed this from Christ's physical return to his own version of an "invisible return" of Christ to the Earth. He joined forces with a publisher Barbour and together they published he magazine The Herald of the Morning. In 1877 they jointly authored a book Three worlds or Plan of Redemption in which they taught that Christ had already invisibly returned in 1844, and his Kingdom would be set up in 1878 and that believers would be a carried away into Heaven as taught in 1 Corinthians 15:51. In 1879, Russell after parting with Barbour later started his own magazine called the Watchtower and in 1884, founded the Watch Tower Bible and Tract Society, the name we know the organisation by today. Russell married Maria Ackley in 1879, who supported his work speaking on his behalf as well answering for him. However, she eventually divorced him because they were incompatible. Russell was also a speaker and editor and he wrote six volume work called "Studies in the Scriptures". These originally were part of Witness doctrine. However as elements of the Russell's theology changed over the years and the prophetic declarations of Russell failed to come to pass, the Watch Tower Society decided to withdraw from circulation all seven volumes of Studies in the Scriptures. The movement began to spread and in 1909, Russell moved the headquarters to Brooklyn New York that became the Brooklyn Tabernacle. Russell died in 1916 and the movement was taken over by Joseph Francis Rutherford. Under Rutherford, the Witnesses grew and called themselves the Jehovah Witnesses in 1931.

Question

Who was Charles Russell and what did he believe?

_____

_____

_____

Beliefs of the Jehovah Witnesses

Jehovah witnesses say that Christianity fell into apostasy when it became the official religion of the Roman Empire under Empire Constantine. They believe that God chose Charles Russell to restore the true religion through his teaching and through their magazines Watchtower and Awake. Like all sects and cults, their doctrines are heretical and contradict the teachings of the Bible on essential Christian Doctrines. They do not observe celebrations such as Christmas, Easter or birthdays, which they believe have pagan origins that are not compatible with Christianity. Members commonly refer to their body of beliefs as "the Truth", and adherents consider themselves to be "in the Truth". Jehovah's Witnesses consider secular society to be morally corrupt and under the influence of Satan, and limit their social interaction with non-Witnesses.

God,

Jehovah's Witnesses believe that there is only one God, the Father almighty. His personal name is Jehovah. They do not believe in the Trinity. Instead, they are strict monotheists, Jehovah is the Supreme Being:

"Is Jehovah a trinity? –three persons in one God? No Jehovah, the Father is the only true God (John 17:3, Mark 12:29), Jesus is his first born son, and he is subject to God (1 Corinthians 11:3). The father is greater than the son (John 14:28), The Holy Spirit is not a person; it is God's active force (Genesis 1:2, Acts 2:1-5) (Watch Tower Bible and Tract Society, What does God require of us?

Jesus

Jehovah Witnesses believe that Jesus is the Son of God, a created being. They believe that he previously existed as the Archangel

Michael. He later took human form as a man like any other person, except that he was sinless at birth and remained so throughout his earthly life. Jehovah's Witnesses do not believe in the bodily resurrection of Christ. They believe that after the crucifixion, Christ died and was resurrected as an invisible, non-material, spirit creature. They believe that Jesus appeared on earth after his resurrection in a special body that Jehovah created for him:

"Jehovah God raised him from the dead not as a human son, but as a mighty immortal spirit son..." ("Let God be True"- Watch Tower Bible Tract Society).

The Holy Spirit:

The Holy Spirit they believe, is not a separate entity, but is simply a force: the method by which God interacts with the world.

The Bible

The Jehovah witnesses claim to believe the Bible as the Word of God, when in reality they corrupt the scriptures to suit their own doctrines. Charles Russell adopted many of the beliefs of the Adventists and brought these beliefs to his study of the Bible. The Jehovah Witnesses began a translation of their own version of the Bible in 1950 that was completed around 1961, called the New World Translation of the Scriptures. The Witnesses claim that this is an accurate and honest translation of the scriptures. However, on close examination it is a mistranslation of the Greek text, deliberately leaving out and adding words and verses to suit Watchtower theology and beliefs. The witnesses also teach that one cannot interpret the Bible for themselves, but need the assistance and guidance of the books put out by the Watch Tower Society:

"We all need help to understand the bible and we cannot find the scriptural guidance we need outside the "faithful and discreet slave" organisation." Watchtower, 2/15/81.19.

Question

What do the Jehovah Witnesses believe about God, Jesus, and the Holy Spirit?

___

___

___

Salvation (Grace vs. Works)

Jehovah Witness believe that two groups of people will be saved, the 144,000 who will reign with Christ in Heaven and the remainder of the saved who will live with Christ on the Earth. The 144,00 will live in Christ in Heaven, these are the elect and truly saved. Those who feel in their hearts that they are elect "anointed" can partake of the Communion service which Jehovah Witnesses have once a year. Those who are not elect, "anointed" will remain on the Earth and will live with Christ on Earth:

"They have been promised everlasting life on earth including the privilege of subduing, beautifying and populating the earth, if they as Jehovah Witnesses prove their faithfulness to him before the war of Armageddon."("Let God be True")

Jehovah Witnesses claim to believe in salvation by grace through Faith in Jesus Christ. In reality, though their religion promotes a works salvation with people being required to attend up to five meetings a week and do endless evangelism. For a person to be saved they must accept the teachings of the governing body of the witnesses and their interpretation of scriptural doctrines. They must also be baptised as a Jehovah and get involved in the work of prompting the religion. They also believe that to be saved one must have the correct knowledge about God Jehovah and Jesus his son.

Hell

They totally deny the existence of Hell. Satan is regarded as having created the concept of Hellfire in order to turn people against God. They believe that hell is the "common grave of mankind" where people go when they die. They are not conscious there. Unbelievers simply cease to exist at death. Believers remain in death until the resurrection:

"The doctrine of a burning hell where the wicked are tormented eternally after death cannot be true for four reasons: 1. Because it is wholly unscriptural: 2 it is unreasonable: 3 It is contrary to God's love; and it is repugnant to justice" ("Let God be True").

Question

What do Jehovah Witnesses believe about Salvation and Hell?

_____

_____

Man's Soul

Jehovah's Witnesses believe that a person is the soul but this soul is not immortal and ceases to exist when a person dies. When the time comes for God to resurrect them from the dead, He will create a new body for them from his memory:

"At death man's spirit, his life-force which is sustained by breathing, goes out" It no longer exists...When they are dead, both humans and animals are in the same state of complete unconsciousness...that the soul live son after death is a lie started by the devil"("You can Live Forever")

144,000

Jehovah Witnesses believe that only 144,000 people will enter Heaven and live with God. The rest of the worthy elect will live Christ on the Earth:

"Who and how many are able to enter into the Kingdom? The Revelation limits it to 144,000, the number that become a part of the Kingdom and stand on mount Zion."("Let God be True.")

Practices of Jehovah Witnesses

The practices and work activities of the Jehovah Witnesses is directed by the Watch Tower Bible and Tract Society in Brooklyn New York , its governing body who they call the faithful and discreet slave" (Mathew 24:4). From there comes all its polices, doctrines and practices which filter down to the local Kingdom Hall elders and congregations. Any form of criticism or dissent by any member of the Jehovah Witnesses is treated as a serious offence and results in disfellowship. Witnesses are taught not to think for themselves about the Bible or any issue. They must receive the teaching and Bible interpretations given them by their leaders as the very Word of God to them.

Evangelism - The Jehovah witnesses stress evangelism as a major part of their religion. The witnesses have what they call Regular Pioneers. They commit themselves to preach the gospel for at least 840 hours a year, 70 hours a month, 17.5 hours a week. Auxiliary Pioneers do 50 hours a month for one or more consecutive months.

	Table showing Jehovah Witnesses activities in the UK 2009							
	Population	Witnesses	Ratio To 1	Baptised	Congregation	Preaching hours	Bible Studies	Memorial attendance
Great Britain	59,842,108	133,900	447	2,932	1,521	21,237,742	55,473	223,432

Kingdom Hall – meeting place of Witnesses, where they teach, study and plan their strategy of evangelism. They meet once a year to celebrate the Lord's Evening Meal (communion), where only a select few are allowed to participate. The Kingdom Hall is used for bible studies and fellowship in the week. This is the only place where members have an active social life with other people. Jehovah Witnesses.

Studying and reading the Bible - Jehovah witnesses devote themselves to studying the Bible and attend as much as five teaching sessions a week at the Kingdom Hall!

Birthdays and Holidays – Jehovah Witnesses do not celebrate birthdays or holidays such as thanksgiving, Christmas and Easter. They believe that these are pagan in origin and it would be sinful to recognise and celebrate them.

Disfellowshipping – The Jehovah Witnesses practice what is called disfellowshipping. This means that a person in the religion can be ostracised/ excommunicated from the group if they break any of the laws and rules of the organisation. Disfellowshipping is a serious issue among Witnesses. Those who have been put out of the fellowship are not allowed to talk or go near another Jehovah Witness. Witnesses themselves are not allowed to talk or have any association with a person who has been put out of the fellowship. Any form of contact with them results in the disfellowshipping of the guilty member.

No Involvement in politics and no Blood Transfusions – The world system is evil and corrupt, so Witnesses do not get involved in politics, they do not vote or go to war. Jehovah's Witnesses forbid their members to have blood transfusions for themselves or their children, claiming that this is the same as eating blood that is forbidden in the Bile. It is a sad fact that many Witnesses have died because of this belief and practice.

Question:

List down the main practises of the Jehovah Witnesses

What Jehovah Witness Believe and their objections Against Christianity

Christianity is corrupted and those who are Christians do not follow the true teachings of Jehovah. The witnesses do not even see themselves as part of Protestant Christianity! In one article entitled six myths about Christianity, they outline their reasons why they believe traditional Christianity is false.

Jehovah Witnesses believe that Charles Russell was the servant of Jehovah chosen to restore the true Christian Faith to the world and bring it back to correct doctrine.

The doctrine of the trinity and Hell fire are inventions of the early Church and not in the bible. Early Christians introduced these doctrines after the death of the apostles.

Jesus is not the Son of God, nor is He God but the archangel Michael.

The Holy Spirit is not God, but a force that emanates from God.

The only True reliable translation is the New World Translation of the bible.

How to Respond to Jehovah's Witnesses

i. **The life and revelations of Charles Russell** - point out to the Witnesses the inconsistencies of the life, prophecies and teachings of their founder Charles Russell. Firstly, his prophetic declarations about Christ return have not been fulfilled. If he is a true prophet of God why has his prophecies proved false? The scriptures clearly teach us that any prophet who gives a prophecy and it does not come to pass is to be ignored: Deuteronomy 18:22 *"When a prophet speaketh in the name of the LORD, if the thing follow not, nor come to pass, that is the thing which the LORD hath not spoken, but the prophet hath spoken it presumptuously: thou shalt not be afraid of him."* Also refer them to other scriptures such as Jeremiah 23:21-22, and Jesus' teaching in Matthew 7:15, 24:11, 2 Peter 2:1. Secondly, if Russell was God's anointed servant and his writings are special revelation given to restore the truth, why has the Watch Tower removed his writings from circulation?

ii. **Since Jehovah Witnesses use their version of the Bible to teach and preach from, you need to show them how it is an erroneous interpretation of the Bible.** Firstly point out that Pastor Russell was wrong in the above, therefore his revelations and teachings are most likely to be wrong on doctrines such as the soul and Hell. Secondly, the scriptures clearly teach us that if anyone preaches another gospel to the one Paul preached he is cursed (Galatians 1:6, 8-9). Also quote the scripture to them in 2 Peter 1:20-21: *"Knowing this first that no prophecy of the **scripture is of any private interpretation**. For the prophecy came not in old time by the will of man: but holy men of God **spake as they were moved by the Holy Ghost**."* How does this fit in with Witness doctrine and their claims about Pastor Russell? Thirdly, their version of the bible came into being in 1961, so the world had to wait until then for a true translation. What happened before this date to the millions who believed on the KJV of the bible? Fourthly, of the six men who formed the committee for the translation of the New World Bible five of them had no formal training in Hebrew or

Greek, the languages of the Bible. How can they then presume to determine what its words mean? For further answers to Jehovah Witness objections to Christianity and the Bible, go to chapter four for explanations that are more detailed.

From these brief introductions to atheistic and theistic worldviews, you can clearly see how Satan has blinded people into believing irrational and incredible beliefs. How can men deny the existence of God, when there is such an abundance of evidence of His existence within and around them (Romans 1:18-28). How can people believe that the Qu'ran and Muhammed are God's final revelation to mankind, when the Bible predates and supersedes these revelations spiritually and morally? How can people believe that there is no soul in man, and no Hell for the wicked? People seriously believe these errors. Apologetics helps us help them find the true God. Apologetics helps us lead them out of the maze of these erroneous beliefs to find the living and true God. In the final chapter, we will look at how to respond to, help these groups of out of these errors, and lead them into the truth of Christianity.

Chapter Four
Responding To Different Worldviews

In this final chapter, we will look at how to approach and share the gospel with people of different worldviews and how to respond to their objections against Christianity. Our aim in Apologetics is to defend our Faith and to persuade men and women of other faiths to embrace Christ as Lord and Saviour. We want to free people from their deceptions and help them find salvation in Jesus Christ alone. Apologetics is ultimately about removing the spiritual and intellectual obstacles Satan has put in the hearts and minds of men, that stop them from seeing the truth (2 Corinthians 4:4). In this chapter, we will look at two important ways we are to respond to people with different worldviews. Firstly how we practically go about evangelising to them, and secondly how to respond to their objections against the Christian Faith.

1. Responding to Other worldviews: Principles and Practise:

i. Adopt a Biblical Method of Persuasion:

"And the servant of the Lord must **not strive**; but be **gentle** unto all men, apt to **teach, patient, In meekness instructing** those **that oppose themselves**; if God peradventure will give them repentance to the acknowledging of the truth." 2 Timothy 2:24

When evangelising to people of different worldviews, it is important that we develop the attitudes Paul outlines in 2 Timothy 2: 24. Apologetics is not just about knowledge and being able to refute other worldviews. It is also about having the right attitude, emotions and spiritual virtues with that knowledge to be able to persuade others that their viewpoint is wrong. In other words, we must have the right heart attitude as well as the right knowledge to persuade people to embrace Jesus. Apologetics is not about ranting and raving about how wrong someone else is. This approach builds up walls of resistance in the person you are trying to reach, and it is a bad witness to those who watch you witness to them. Some people think that talks and discussions have to be heated exchanges. However, it does not have to be like that. Jesus, Paul, Peter, Apollos all reasoned and debated with their opponents as we saw in lesson one, but they did it in the RIGHT SPIRIT AND ATTITUDE. Paul reasoned calmly with the Jews and did not lose his temper. A discussion with an unbeliever should be like discussions in a college forum, where both parties are given the opportunity to air their views and beliefs. One person expresses their beliefs whilst the other is quietly listening, and taking note of what the person is saying. After a while, they then present their beliefs and show the flaws in the other person's argument. Remember this when you go out to evangelise unbelievers. To do effective Apologetics in Evangelism you must have the right spiritual attitudes as well as the knowledge to be able to answer and refute the charges being made against your Faith. As a Christian, you *are there to help another person come to truth in Jesus, so your motivation should be love (1 Corinthians 13:1-3)*. Recognise that the person is in spiritual darkness and unless God gives them light and repentance, they cannot see the truth. Your role is to present the truth to them, God's role is to drive this truth home into their minds and hearts bringing conviction and repentance (2 Timothy 2:24). In 2 Timothy 2:24, Paul lists the spiritual qualities we must possess when persuading others to come to the Jesus.

"And the servant of the Lord ...

a. **"must not strive."** The word means those who "who engage in a war of words, to quarrel, wrangle"

Defending your faith and showing other people the weaknesses of their beliefs is not arguing and striving with them. As we mentioned above it should done in a calm manner, each giving the other person the opportunity to share their beliefs. You can control the interactions you have with unbelievers with your spirit and your attitude. If you practice peace, calmness and self-control it will begin to affect how the other person interacts and responds to you. Once you begin to talk to someone and they open up to you, you might want to say to them, *"shall we sit down here for a moment and discuss this further?"*, or *"would you like to go for a coffee and talk more about this further"* or *"can we arrange a time to meet up so I can go through some of your concerns about Christianity?"*

b. **"gentle unto all men"**, means "mild or kind" This relates to the tone, the manner in which you interact with another person. Is your spirit too rough or harsh?

c. **"able to teach"** – to do this you must have knowledge of your faith and worldviews of others

d. **"patient"** means enduring of ill, i.e. forbearing:--patient. You are going to have to listen to lot of false teachings, do not be impatient however, but wait and exercise patience. This virtue will persuade them just as much as your knowledge will.

e. **"in meekness"** means gentleness, mildness, meekness, humbleness – do not show off your knowledge, present it to them in a humble spirit, as one who also had to come to the truth - Titus 3:1

f. **"instructing those who oppose themselves"** instruct means, to cause one to learn, to train up a child, i.e. educate. Remember unbelievers are in darkness, and have erroneous views about God and Heaven. Your job is to instruct them in the truth

g. **"that God would give them repentance"** – realise that only God can bring your words home to them and give them repentance to turn from the error of their ways. Pray for God to give them repentance

ii. Recognise the Society and the Political Atmosphere in which you live. The values of society are Humanist in nature, and Humanists are opposed to religion especially Christianity.

"Behold, I send you forth as sheep in the midst of wolves: be ye therefore wise as serpents, and harmless as doves." Matthew 10:16

We are living in a society that is hostile to Christianity and denies absolute truths in the areas of beliefs and morals. So we need to do what Jesus said and be wise and not allow ourselves to be caught up in argumentative political discussions. This is why the spiritual qualities Paul listed above are important in evangelism. When you adopt the right spiritual attitudes coupled with knowledge of the truth, you make it difficult for people to accuse you of being harsh, dogmatic and judgemental. You need to recognise that you are challenging the worldviews of Western Society. Your Christian Faith and beliefs will seem harsh and outdated to people who are basically Humanists. To people of other faiths such as Muslims you will seem blasphemous! Jesus said in Matthew 10:6 that we must use wisdom and be harmless towards the people we evangelise to. Our society is hostile to the Christian worldview and is looking for an opportunity to label and criticise Christians as fundamentalist, intolerant people. We should adopt the style that Jesus had when he preached. He lived in a similar society. In His day, the Roman emperors ruled and it was politically incorrect to say that you were a King or even Divine, since only Caesar was king and divine. To say either of these about yourself was to commit treason, a crime punishable by death. Jesus also lived amongst religious Pharisees who sought constantly to trap him so that they could falsely accuse Him. Recall the incident when the Pharisees tried to trap Him by asking Him the question of whether taxes should be paid to Caesar (Matthew 22:17). Jesus avoided their traps until it was time for Him to be crucified. Pray for wisdom when you evangelise and have a gentle and mild spirit towards the people you witness to.

II. Know how to Open up a Conversation and Maintain an Atmosphere of calm, peaceful discussion with an unbeliever. Below is a pattern you may wish to follow.

i. Begin by stating who you are and that you are a Christian and what Church you are from:

"Good (*morning, afternoon, etc.*) my name is _____ (and this is - _____ - *if you have a witnessing partner*). I am (We are) from _____ (*the church you are from*) and we were just out doing some visiting from our church and wondered if you attended church anywhere?" No matter what they say, your answer is going to be "fantastic." If they do attend church every week, then again say, "Great where do you attend church?" (*Wait for their answer.*) If they do not attend church, you say, "Fantastic", you are just the type of person we are looking for." (*This makes them feel relaxed.*) Then say, "By the way, what is your name?" (*Remember to ask their name and use if frequently*) **Mark, let me ask you a very important question. If you should die today, are you 100% certain that you would go to heaven?"**

<u>*Always*</u> *ask this question <u>immediately</u> even if they tell you they do not have time.*

Possible responses:

- "I'm not sure"

Then say, "You need to be sure about such an important matter. God has given us the Bible as the spiritual guide. It tells us the requirements to enter God's Heaven. Let me go through them with you now" >>> the Ten Commandments:

- "Yes I will go to Heaven"

Then go through the Ten Commandments with them "Are you a Good Person, good enough for Heaven?"

However if they respond in the following two ways:

- "I don't believe in Heaven or Hell I'm an atheist/humanist/evolutionist

- I am a Muslim/Jehovah Witness

Then an opportunity has been created for you to enter into a calm, peaceful reasonable discussion with them about their beliefs. Then ask them in a peaceful tone

ii. "That is very interesting, could you just explain to me why you believe there is no God or why you are a Muslim?"

iii. **Listen to them share their beliefs for about 10 minutes**, nodding and showing that you are listening. At the same time discern what their beliefs are, secular humanist, evolutionist, atheist, Muslim, Jehovah witness.

iv. **After they have explained their position,** they will normally have criticisms against the Christian faith or explain to you their worldview. This is how you respond to them:

Criticisms/objectives against the Christian Faith

"I can see you have some concerns about the Christian Faith which I would like to answer and help you overcome" – then respond to them using the responses we went through in the book.

OR

Humanist/atheists/evolutionist worldviews

"**I understand you have beliefs about God, the world and the universe.** However, some of the things you say do not fit in with the facts of the world and universe. For instance you say that...."

Then go through with them the issues we raised against the different worldviews, and argue the case for God's existence and why the Christian worldview is the only one that makes sense of the facts of the world, and the universe.

OR

Muslim/Jehovah Witnesses

If the person is a Muslim or Jehovah Witness, gently challenge them to see if they have always practised their faith 100% of the time and are they sure that they will go to Heaven of dwell on Earth with the saints. Ask the Muslims have they kept all the commandants in the Bible and the Qu'ran? Do they practise their faith 100%? Explain to them that *God is going to judge them*, not their religion or organisation (Hebrews 9:26), and unless they are pure and holy they will not enter Heaven, paradise or dwell with the saints on Earth. Ask the Jehovah Witness are they 100% sure that the teachings of their founder is correct compared to 3,000 years of written Biblical information contained in the Bible. Point out to the JW that he is putting the fate of his eternal soul at risk by following the beliefs of one man who already made serious mistakes when it came to his prophetic utterances. Ask the JW is he a good witness, good enough to please Jehovah whom he serves? Will Jehovah receive him or will he be with those who are annihilated when they die?

v. **Present the Gospel to them of Jesus Christ dying for their sins and the sins of the whole world**. Explain the fall of men, the need for redemption, that all have sinned and how Christ paid for our sins on the Cross of Calvary. Then explain to them how to receive Him through Repentance and Faith.

2. Responding to the objections and challenging the worldviews of Secular Humanists, Evolutionists, New Atheists, Muslims and Jehovah Witnesses

We noted in chapters two and three that atheists and people are other faiths have objections towards Christianity. We listed some of these objections in those chapters. In this section, we will respond in these objections in more detail.

Responding to objections of Secular Humanists
- see chapter 2, page 26-27 humanists objections to Christianity

Denial of the Existence of God and the Supernatural, see page 26.

Secular humanists, evolutionists and new atheists argue that God does not exist. You need to show them that although they believe this, they cannot be 100% that God does not exist! To say that they are sure that He does not exist, is to claim that they know the total knowledge there is available in the universe, which is absurd. There are many things they do not know about the universe. Show them that their statement "there is no God" is not a statement of fact, but of faith. It is a statement of faith because they have already admitted they do not know everything, and part of what they do not know could include the existence of God! Help them see that their position of atheism is actually a faith position. They *believe in the non-existence of God*, because they do not have absolute certainty that He does not exist! Present to them the arguments for God's existence, and how these arguments put together are a strong case for the existence of God. *The argument from design,* - the order of the world and its complexity shows us that there has to be an intelligent mind behind it especially when we consider the information stored in Deoxyribonucleic Acid (DNA). Where did this information come from? We know from experience that information comes from intelligence, therefore we can safely conclude that an infinite intelligence had to be responsible for the complex information we find in DNA and in the Universe. *The moral argument-* shows them that all men have a moral law inside them. Where did this law come from? Evolution cannot give us a valid reason why we should evolve to be moral beings. The only reasonable explanation is that this moral law was put within us by a supernatural moral governor; God. *The Cosmological argument-* that everything that exists has a cause for its existence. The universe exists and had a beginning so something must have caused it to come into existence. That something is God (Genesis 1:1, 2, John 1:1, Colossians 1:14) Now the atheist is a reasonable, rational person who claims to examine the evidence. Ask them then that if all these arguments for the existence of God were presented in a court of law, do they think that a jury weighing all this evidence would conclude that God does not exist? Of course not! The evidence weighs in favour of the existence of God. Challenge them: "why friend do you deny your own reason and intelligence by trying to argue there is no God?" Show them that the Bible already gives them the answer why they do this. It says that they deny God's existence because they want to continue in sin and do not want to be accountable to God (Rom.ans 1:18-21). Ask them: "Friend is this not the real reason you say there is no God?" Then call on them to repent and ask God for mercy and forgiveness, and He will pardon and forgive them!

Religion and Christianity is harmful to society see page 26

Secular humanists and the new atheists argue that Christianity and religion is harmful to society and to individuals. When we evangelise atheists we must show them the truth about Christianity and its contributions to society and the well-being of individuals. We admit to them that many wicked crimes have been committed in the name of Christianity. However, this does not mean that Christianity is bad in itself. Rather it shows that those who use Christianity for these ends are bad and wicked. The life and teachings of the founder of Christianity Jesus are based upon love and forgiveness, and reconciliation between God and man, and man and his neighbour. The ethics of Jesus is an ideal ethic for humankind to live by. Explain to them how Christianity has done countless good to western society. It was through Christianity and the Bible that the very foundations of Western Society and Civilisation were built and the reason it prospered. The contributions of Christianity to the world are too numerous to mention. Christianity was behind much of the Western Scientific discoveries we take for granted today. Christianity has been at the forefront of humanitarian causes, such the abolition of slavery and child labour, literacy programmes, the building of, hospitals and the provision of orphanages for children. Wilberforce who fought for the abolition of slavery was also an advocate of animal welfare. William and Catherine booth did much work to alleviate child suffering on the streets of London and in the factories of Victorian Britain. It was because Christians took the teachings of Jesus in Matthew 25:45, literally "Whatever you did not do for one of the least of these, you did unto me" that hospital and welfare programmes were developed for the sick and needy. Christianity with its emphasises on the dignity of the human being was behind most initiatives aimed at alleviating suffering, such as the civil rights movement, prison reform, workers rights and women's rights. Christianity far from being harmful to humanity has civilised and uplifted it!

Morality and Ethics is not based on God or the Bible, Human beings develop their own morality and ethics see page 27

When a secular humanists, evolutionists or new atheists say that moral values do not have their basis in a supernatural being, you need to show them the absurdity of this position. If ethics is relative and situational, and there is no such thing as moral absolutes, then the Hitler, Stalin, the 9/11 terrorist attacks are not "wrong" because "wrongness" does not exist and everyone has a right to their own subjective moral standards. This means that a thief who believes in stealing as a way of life has the right to go into your home and rob you of your possession. It also means that someone has to the right to treat you unfairly or slander you if they wish, because values and behaviour is all subjective. Challenge the humanist by asking them this question: "Why do you feel angry if a person steals from you? Why do you have a sense of justice and desire retribution for the wrong committed against you? Why do human beings possess this moral sense?" The reason is that there really is a moral law within all of us that tells us that the actions of others are right or wrong irrespective of what we want to believe with our minds. Challenge the humanist and atheist and show them the absurdity believing that morality is relative! Does the humanist see that if morality is relative and subjective, then everyone is entitled to their own ethical position, which leads to chaos and anarchy? The very fact that the humanist and Christian know that murder, rape and stealing is wrong, is because there is a higher moral law that we all recognise that transcends culture. So morality is based on an absolute, and that absolute is God Himself the originator of moral law. Explain to the atheist/evolutionist that if there is no God then there cannot be any basis for morality not even a humanist morality! Why? Because the universe has no moral standards. The only law according to evolutionists is the survival of the fittest, so no one has right to invent moral values and impose them on others, and that includes humanists! Show them that there cannot be any logical and rational basis for morality and ethics if there is no God. The Humanist's optimism about humanity is clearly seen to be based in nothing but wishful thinking and is contrary to the very nature of the indifferent, survival of the fittest universe he espouses.

Once you have shown them that morality cannot be subjective and refute the false belief that there are no absolute moral standards, introduce them to the Christian morality as enshrined in the Ten Commandments and the teachings of Jesus, showing them that these provide us with the right moral framework to govern society and the world. Then ask them to measure their lives against these standards to see if they are good people. Then Introduce Jesus who has fulfilled all these standards on their behalf and saved them from the penalty of breaking these commandments.

Responding to Evolutionist objections against Christianity

"Science can explain the world without reference to God so God does not exist" page 31

Evolutionists and atheists will tell you that because science can understand many of the laws of the universe and how it works, that this makes belief in God redundant. One reason they say this is because there was a time when men attributed natural things to the gods of religion. Many natural events such as storms, eclipses of the sun, natural disasters and sicknesses were attributed to the work of gods and spirits. Evolutionists argue that now we can explain these phenomenon without recourse to the gods, then the gods do not exist! It is true that many natural events were falsely attributed to God, but this by no means makes belief in God obsolete. Science and religion are not in opposition to each other. Indeed many of the great discoveries of modern science have been done by scientists who were committed Christians. Although science can give us explanations of how things work in the material world, it cannot and is unable to answer the ultimate questions about the universe such as why is there a universe in the first place? Why is it made the way it is? How did it come into being? How will the universe end? How did life on Earth begin? How will life on Earth end? These are beyond the ability of scientific investigation and are questions only theologians can answer. Therefore, for evolutionists and humanists to say that science can give us a total explanation for the way things are is nonsense. Explain to evolutionists that many secular scientists acknowledge that here are some questions science cannot answer. The famous evolutionary biologist Steven Gould was a scientist who recognised this truth. He developed his idea of NOMA- Non-overlapping Magisteria. This says that science deals with empirical factual information and religion deals with ultimate philosophical questions and both fields of enquiry do not overlap. What Gould was saying was that science could not give a total answer to the ultimate questions that we have about the universe, only religion can do this. So religion and science are two very different fields of knowledge dealing with different questions and issues. If this great evolutionary biologist recognised the limitations of his science, then the truth is that science cannot give us total answers and explanations about life, the world and the universe! Explain to evolutionists that the only answer that makes sense of the universe on the scientific and philosophical level, is that there is indeed a supernatural creator who created it for a purpose and who designed the laws that govern it.

The Earth is billions of years old, and this proves the Bible account the date of the Earth to be incorrect, page 31

Evolutionists often argue that rocks and fossils are millions of years old and that this proves that the Bible account of creation is false. They use various methods to date the age of the Earth and a popular one is Carbon 14 dating. However, carbon 14 method is unreliable and is based on false assumptions about the state and conditions of the Earth over time. When living animals eat food or plants and take in carbon dioxide, they end up with tiny amounts (i.e. 1 in 1,000,000,000,000 atoms) of carbon-14 – a radioactive isotope - inside them. When they die, they stop taking in C-14. The amount of C-14 isotope halves by decaying every 5730 years (plus or minus 40 years), i.e. its half-life is 5730 years. If you can measure the amount of C-14 in something, then you can estimate its age based on assumptions about the original amounts it contained and decay rates. *This is reasonably good for things that died within a few thousand years, but after 57,3000 years* (10 half-lives), the amount of C-14 remaining in something is: ½ x ½ x ½ x ½ x½ x ½ x ½ x ½ x ½ x ½ = 1/1024 = *0.00098 of the* original tiny (1 in 1000 billion) amount. *The amount after 57, 3000 years is theoretically not detectable. The fact that samples contain any C-14 is good evidence that they are not millions of years old.* In reality, carbon dating before 5,000 years is unrealistic. Evolutionists also claim that fossilisation occurs over, millions of years. This has been found to be untrue. They now know that fossilisation can occur as early as 40 years, one generation. The true age of the Earth is thousands of years old as the Bible teaches and not millions of years old as evolutionists teach. *("Creation Points, Creation and Evolution.")*

Man evolved from apes and is not a special creation, page 31

We have already mentioned that there is no proof for human evolution. No fossil records that are transitional forms demonstrating that human evolution took place. Inform the evolutionist of the many frauds that have been put forward by those who wanted to prove evolution to be true. Ask them why if evolution is true have we been presented over the last 100 years with fossils that claimed to be missing links but were hoaxes? Some of these include the 1865 Neanderthal Man unearthed in Germany said to be the missing link, now most experts agree was a member of the human race; Piltdown Man of 1912 said to be the missing link, now proven to be a hoax, a 4000 year human skull glued to an orang-utan's jaw, Nutcracker man of 1859 found in Africa and said by National geographic to be the missing link, experts now agree to be the skull of an extinct ape and Lucy of 1974 which most experts agree is not a missing link at all. Also, point out to the evolutionist that if man was the product of evolution a "grown-up germ" why do human beings think so highly of themselves? Why do they celebrate their birthdays, special occasions, pamper and groom themselves, are concerned with human dignity, freedom, equality, health,? Why do they make such a distinction between themselves and the animals that they are supposed to be related to? The only rational explanation for this is that man is more than an animal and knows and senses it. The Bible teaches us that man is created in the image and likeness of God (Genesis 1:26-28) and although fallen man still has the sense that he is a higher being than the animals around him.

Responding to the New Atheism's Objections against Christianity

The universe is the type of universe you would expect if there no God, page 35

Atheists such as Dawkins point out that the competitive struggle for survival in nature, storms and natural disasters show that the world is a random, chaotic place with no order or divine providence. This is really an argument against God's existence due to the existence of evil and disorder in the world. This argument states that if there is a wise loving God ruling over the universe, why is the universe the way it is with babies being born deformed, earthquakes, starvation, disease, war and famine? All these evils prove that there is no God governing the universe! We need to explain to atheists that although evil and chaos seem to reign at times, this does not mean that there is no God. Explain to them the Christian doctrine of sin and why evil exists in the first place. In the beginning, God created the world and mankind perfect and gave man ruler-ship over the planet (Genesis 1:26-28). However, this ruler-ship and dominion could only be successfully practised if mankind remained in relationship with God. Unfortunately, we chose to sin and disconnect ourselves and creation from God. This means that the universe is now in a state of disorder and separation from the source of power and life that brought it into being in the first place; God. This is the reason the universe, world and mankind is the way it is today. Explain to them *the principle of contingency,* that everything is dependent on everything else in the animal kingdom, world, and in the universe. It is the same with the creation and God. God is the source of life and power for the creation He has made. However, for that life and power from God to flow into the world and mankind, there has to be a connection between God, creation and mankind. *Because we have sinned and cut ourselves off from God, His power to protect, heal and regenerate his creation and mankind has been extremely limited.* The result is that there is decay, sickness, death and chaos in the world and in the human race. Just as we on the Earth are dependent upon the

Sun to survive, so we are dependent upon God to survive. However if the Earth moved just one degree away from the Sun, the whole planet would freeze and life on Earth could not be sustained. In a similar way, we are like the Earth moving away from Sun, God. What we are seeing in the universe is a creation that has lost vital, living contact and power with its creator and as a result, it is in a process of decay and death, because of man's sin. This is why the universe is the way it is. However, the Bible tells us that there will come a time when God will make a new heavens and a new Earth (Revelation 21:2).

Religious beliefs causes people to suspend rational thinking, and it is opposed to science, page 35

Many people you evangelise to, will be new atheists. One of the false charges they make against the Christian Faith is that Christians are taught to suspend reason and blindly believe the Bible. They argue that religious belief and science are opposed to each other. They try to make science and religion at odds with each other as if to belief in God means you have to reject science and the scientific method of investigation. This is false. The truth is that modern science owes many of its great discoveries to deeply religious men who were Christians and scientists. These scientists were men who saw science and religion as related to each other. As Christians, they believed that God created the universe and set laws and principles that men were to investigate and discover. In doing this, they were giving glory and honour to the great God and His creation. It was their belief in God that motivated and inspired them to learn about the natural world. Far from inhibiting scientific investigation of the natural world, Christianity encouraged it! To say that Christianity inhibits thinking is just a blatant lie. Scientists who were Christians included men such as **Nicholas Copernicus (1473-1543)**, the astronomer who put forward the first mathematically based system of planets going around the Sun, **Sir Francis Bacon (1561-1627)** the philosopher who is known for establishing the scientific method of inquiry based on experimentation and inductive reasoning. Bacon was a theist who denied atheism, yet the atheists of today have taken his scientific method and are trying to use it to disprove God's existence! Other great figures include men such as **Isaac Newton (1642-1727)**, who made great discoveries in optics, mechanics, mathematics, and astronomy. He too was a devout Christian. In his Principia, he wrote: "The most beautiful system of the sun, planets, and comets, could only proceed from the counsel and dominion on an intelligent and powerful Being." The list could go on to include **Robert Boyle** who made discoveries in gases and chemistry, **Michael Faraday (1791-1867)**, whose work on electricity and magnetism not only revolutionized physics, but led to much of our lifestyles today, which depends on them (including computers and telephone lines). Many atheists have believed the lie promoted by Dawkins and the new atheists about the relationship between science and religion. Explain to them the truth, and show them how Christianity prompted and advanced science not hindered it.

Religious beliefs are memes, mind viruses passed on from one generation to another, page 35

Richard Dawkins in his book, "The selfish Gene" put forward the idea that religious beliefs were a form of mind virus, which he called a "meme". These viruses are cultural and religious viruses of the mind that are passed on from one generation to the next. Explain to those who promote this view, that there is no scientific evidence for the existence of memes. If an atheist tries to use this argument and talk about religious belief in such terms, ask them do they have any scientific observable evidence to prove the existence of memes? They will not have any evidence because they do not exist!

Religious indoctrination of Children is child abuse, page 35-36

Richard Dawkins argues in his book "The God Delusion" that religious parents, who bring up their children to believe in their religious doctrines, are mentally abusing their children. That to teach and enforce religious beliefs upon Children is a form of child abuse. Many atheists will use this argument and say that religion is bad for children. It is important to let these people know that *Dawkins has absolutely no evidence for this*. Dawkins is constantly demanding scientific evidence from others for the claims that they make about religion, yet here he makes a statement that has no scientific evidence to back it up! The truth is the opposite what Dawkins says. In one of the largest studies of its kind, the University of North Carolina at Chapel Hill examined the role of religion in the lives of nearly 2500 adolescents. The adolescents indicated the level of their indoctrination (i.e. frequency of church attendance) and importance of religion, along with a number of activities that they have or have not participated in. What the data showed was that religiously indoctrinated youth are much less involved with illegal substances, alcohol abuse, criminal and violent activities, and have fewer problems in school. Dawkins's hypothesis that religious indoctrination is bad for children has been soundly falsified. In fact, children who never attend church or feel that religion is not important, display far more symptoms of real child abuse than those who are subject to frequent religious indoctrination. Not only do children of religious people behave better than their irreligious peers, they are also happier children. A study from the University of British Columbia found, "Children who were more spiritual were happier. Spirituality accounted for between 3 and 26% of the unique variance in children's happiness depending on the measures." (*Holder, M. D., B. Coleman, and J. M. Wallace. 2008. Spirituality, Religiousness, and Happiness in Children Aged 8–12 Years.* J Happiness Stud.

Responding to Muslim Objections against Christianity

Muslims deny the Trinity saying it does not make sense, page 80

Muslims and Jehovah witnesses deny the doctrine of the Trinity saying it is unscriptural and illogical. Point out to them what the Bible says about the doctrine of the Trinity since they both claim to believe the Bible. Point out that the very first verse of the Bible Genesis 1:1, the word for "God" is plural-"Elohim," which means "gods" Also when God created man in Genesis 2:6, the word "God" is "Elohim", the plural is used. Show them other scriptures in the Bible that prove that Jesus and the Holy Spirit are Divine. Scriptures in the Old and New Testaments that show that Jesus is God include, Proverbs 30:4, Psalm 2:7-12, Isaiah 9:6, Daniel 7:13-14, John 1:1, Philippians 1:2. Scriptures that show that the Holy Spirit is God include, Genesis 1:2, Job 33:4, Isaiah 63:8-10, Acts 5:3-4, 1 Cor. 2:10-11. Explain to them that Christians do not believe in three gods, but one God who exists in three persons. Just as a triangle has three sides, yet the whole make the one triangle, so God as a Trinity consists of three persons but one Divine nature. Just as man is made up of body, soul and spirit, yet he is one man, God is made up of three persons, different personalities of the one Divine nature. The three persons are not three gods but one God. Muslims often want to know why the doctrine of the Trinity is important for Christians. Explain its importance for the salvation of mankind. Say to them, "we all agree that God is holy and perfect and when we sin against him, we infinitely offend him and will never be able to pay the debt we owe him. However, Jesus who is God became flesh and took upon himself the sins of the whole world when he died upon the cross. He paid back the infinite debt we owed to and infinitely holy God. Only God can satisfy and pacify an offended Holy God. Jesus being God satisfied and pacified the debt humanity owed God and brought us salvation. This is one of the reasons why the doctrine of the trinity is vital to our Christian faith, for without it there cannot be any salvation, for man can never please an infinitely holy God." Then say to the Muslim or Jehovah witness, "So friend, do you believe that your good works and practises can satisfy and appease a Holy God whom you have infinitely offended?" Then offer them Jesus as the payment for their sins asking them to receive Him as their Lord and Saviour.

Muslims deny that Jesus is the Son of God because this would mean that God had relations with a woman, page 48

Some Muslims quoting Sura 112:1-4 think that when Christians say, "Jesus is the son of God" they mean that God fathered Jesus by having physical relations with a woman. I stress some Muslims mistakenly think like this. Explain to them that this is not true as they can clearly read from the gospel of Luke 1:34-35 which they claim to believe. In this scripture, the angel Gabriel visits Mary and tells her how she will supernaturally conceive Jesus in her womb by the power of the Holy Spirit. Also inform them that Sura 112:1-4 is not saying that God fathered Jesus through physical relations with a woman, but is talking in general terms of God not having a son wherever through supernatural means or otherwise. We as Christians never believed or said that God begot a son through relations with a woman and we believe like Muslims that to say so is blasphemy.

Muslims say that salvation is not through Jesus Christ but through works and the forgiveness of Allah, page 48

Say to the Muslim: "You believe that God is holy and righteous. You believe that he has ninety-nine names that demonstrate his power and holiness. You are aware that you are simply a human being, who has done wrong and sinned, yet you hope that your good works on the day of judgement will out-balance your bad works. You are conscious of evil thoughts, emotions desires and actions coming from your heart, mind and emotions and that God watches everything you do. How is it possible then that you and I who are essentially bad can produce anything good in our lives? You believe the Bible, and the Bible teaches that Adam and Eve sinned and we are the descendants of Adam and Eve. The Qur'an says, "To those who believe and do deeds of righteousness hath Allah promised forgiveness and a great reward" (Surah 5:9). Are you doing enough good deeds to receive salvation on the Day of Judgment? Are you doing all you can or are you relaxing in your dedication to Allah? How do you know Allah will forgive you? How do you know if you have done enough good work to please him and earn forgiveness? You cannot answer these questions friend with 100% assurance because your own conscience convicts you of sin and neglect before God. Now we both recognise Jesus to be a great prophet and that he lived a good life. However, He was more that a prophet, He was God in the flesh. He did not sin in thought word or action, He was perfect. He came to die and take our sins upon the cross to make us right with God. Only He being God could satisfy God's justice and righteousness, being perfect and being divine. Only God can satisfy the claims of God. Jesus was God and satisfied the claims of God the Father on behalf of us sinful human beings. You know that you have done wrong; your conscience tells you so. God can never accept you with your imperfect works and imperfect obedience to His commands. Only one who is perfect, fully obedient to the divine commands and God in nature can be acceptable to God. Jesus was that person, and this is why you can only be saved by believing and receiving Him into your life as your Lord and Saviour." Ask them if they would like to receive Jesus into their lives to be their lord and Saviour

Responding to Jehovah Witnesses' objections to Christianity

Jehovah Witness say that Christianity is corrupted and that God had to raise up Charles Russell to restore the true worship of God, page 60

Many of the false sects argue the corruption of Christianity and the need to restore it to its original foundations. Mention this fact to the witnesses that you evangelise. Tell them that there are many sects similar to their own who claim that they have been raised up by God to restore true Christianity to the world. So their message is not new or original. Mormons see themselves as the only true Christians. Explain to them that the *only true measure for the genuineness of Christianity is the Bible itself. Explain to them what the Bible says about itself quoting 2 Timothy 2:15 and 2 Peter. 2; 24.* This last scripture says that the scriptures are not the product of a man's private interpretation or view, but is the result of the direct inspiration of God the Holy Spirit. In other words God wrote the Bible not man! Although it is true that Christians have introduced many things into the Faith that are not biblical, *this does not mean that God raises up men to restore His Church who hold doctrines contrary to His Word, the Bible.* In other words, God does not raise up new "apostles" or "teachers" who teach doctrines contrary to His Word! God's restoration of His Church does not include adding or taking away doctrines found in the Bible (revelation 22:19)! Explain to them that since Charles Russell added new doctrines to the Bible, and the Bible clearly teaches that anyone who does this is cursed (Galatians 1:8-9), then Russell was not a man God raised up! Explain to them that Russell denied the divinity of Christ and the Bible says in 2 John 1:9 that whoever does so has neither the Father nor the Son!

Explain to them that when God chooses to restore Biblical truths to His Church, He raises up *men and women who confirm what is written in the Holy Scripture and they never add or take away the doctrines found in the Scriptures.* The Reformers Martin Luther, John Calvin, and Zwingili, all confirmed what the Bible taught. Every restoration movement God raises up in His Church always restores the practises and doctrines of the early Church found in the book of Acts. Since Russell's doctrines and practices are not scriptural then we can say he is not a true prophet of God; God did not send him. Jesus said He would build his Church and the gates of Hell would not be able to stand against it (Matthew 16:18). Jesus not Charles Russell is the head and keeper of his Church. Ask the JW if he sees this truth and is he willing to embrace Jesus and renounce Charles Russell?

Jehovah Witness deny the Doctrine of the Trinity and Hell, page 60

To evangelise Jehovah witnesses, you must answer their objections with scriptural texts. *All of their objections are doctrinal in nature.* They deny some aspect of Christian Doctrine. When you meet a Jehovah Witness they a will argue that Hell does not exist and that wicked souls are annihilated at death. There are two ways of dealing with this false doctrine. *Firstly*, quote the scriptures that clearly teach on the eternity of Hell torments such as Matthew 18:8, where Jesus talks about being cast into eternal fire, Matthew 25:56

were Jesus says that the wicked will go into eternal punishment, 2 Thessalonians 1:9 where Paul teaches that the enemies of Christ shall suffer eternal destruction, Jude verses 22-23; where He says that those who live sinful lives will be cast into the blackness of darkness forever and the Apostle John in the book of Revelation 20:10 who says that the devil and the false prophet will be cast into the lake of Fire and be tormented forever and ever. So the scriptures clearly teach on the eternity of Hell torments. *Secondly*, teach them that the doctrine of annihilation is based on the false view that God is too compassionate to send people to eternal destruction. Explain to JWs the gravity of sin and its ultimate effect upon the soul of the unrepentant sinner. Every sin you and I do is against and infinite holy God. The only fit punishment for sin is eternal punishment as this satisfies the eternal holy nature of God. If Hell were not eternal, and man was annihilated at death, then he would not be punished for the sins he committed against a Holy eternal God. Explain to the JWs that God who is eternal must punish us eternally in Hell because our sins eternally offends Him and so must reap an eternal punishment. Only a being that was perfect and divine, could satisfy the claims of infinite justice, remove on behalf of others their sins and the punishment due to them for their sins. That being was the second person of the Trinity the lord Jesus Christ who died to pay for our sins on the Cross. Tell them in all kindness that if they do not give up this erroneous and unscriptural teaching and embrace the sacrifice of Christ for their sins, then they will find themselves in an eternal Hell separated from God forever!

Jesus is the archangel Michael and not the son of Go, page 60

Quote the scriptures that clearly teach the Jesus is the Son of God. The Jws teach that Jesus is the archangel Michael. Michael the archangel is mentioned only five times in the Bible (Daniel 10:13, 21; 12:1; Jude 9; Revelation 12:7), and yet never do these passages indicate that he is to be equated with the pre-incarnate Christ, nor with the ascended Jesus. First Thessalonians 4:16 also alludes to "an archangel," and, although the name Michael is not mentioned, this is the passage Jehovah's Witnesses frequently cite as proof of

Jesus being the archangel Michael. Concerning the Second Coming of Christ, Paul wrote: "For the Lord Himself will descend from heaven with a shout, *with the voice of an archangel*, and with the trumpet of God. And the dead in Christ will rise first". Supposedly, since Jesus is described as descending from heaven "with the voice of an archangel," then He must be the archangel Michael. However, this verse does not teach that Jesus is an archangel, but that at His Second Coming *He will be accompanied "with the voice of an archangel." Just as He will be attended "with a shout" and "with the trumpet of God," so will He be accompanied "with the voice of an archangel."* There are two conclusive scriptures you can quote to JWs that Jesus is not an angle but God Himself. The first one is found in Colossians 1:16 that says that all things were created by Him, principalities and powers-these are ranks of angels fallen and elect. The second scripture is found in Hebrews 1:5-13. In this scripture, Paul showed the superiority of Jesus over the angelic beings, and contrasted Him with them. Jesus' superiority over the angels is seen in the fact that the Father spoke to Jesus as His special begotten Son to Whom He gave the seat of honour at His right hand (1:5, 13). Furthermore, the writer of Hebrews indicated that God commanded all angels to worship Jesus (Revelation 5:11-13; Philippians 2:10). Yet, if Jesus were an angel, how could He accept the worship of another "lesser" angels when, according to Revelation 19:10 and 22:8-9, angels do not accept worship, but rather preach the worship of God, and no other? Then invite the JW to receive Jesus into their life as their Lord and Saviour

The Holy Spirit is a force and not God, page 60

This is another one of the blasphemous teachings of the JWs. It is important that when you encounter them and seek to show them the truth, *you always use the scriptures that support the truth.* There are many scriptures that show that the Holy Spirit is a person and is God. The personhood of the Holy Spirit is shown the fact that he can be grieved Ephesians 4:30, I Thessalonians 4:13, insulted Hebrews 10:29, known John 14:17, lied to Acts 5:3, 4, resisted Acts 7:51. The scriptures that show the Holy Spirit is God are seen when

He is referred to as Eternal John 14:16 (Hebrews 9:14), is called God, Acts 5:4, is called Lord, 2 Corinthians 3:17, 18, is from Heaven Matthew 3:16 Mark 1:10 Luke.3:22 John 1:32, and is holy, Matthew 12. Say to the JW in the light of these scriptures how can the Holy Spirit be a mere force? There are too many scriptures that support the Christian doctrine of the personality and deity of the Holy Spirit. A useful point to make when witnessing to JWs is to show them how they have to keep on reinterpreting these scriptures to suit their doctrines. The very fact that they have to do this should show them that there is something wrong with their belief system!

These are some of the ways we can begin to respond to the objections of unbelievers and people of other faiths. It is my prayer that through this book you have gained an awareness of the importance, value and necessity of apologetics to do evangelism in Britain today. Let us go forward armed with this knowledge and deliver men and women from the power of the devil, who are kept captive by him to do his will, and lead them to the true God that loves them, died for them and will save them, once they renounce their errors and embrace His Son Jesus Christ.

NOTES

NOTES

Bibliography

1. Thayer's Greek-English lexicon of the New Testament

2. " " Ibid

3. Contending or the Faith, Phil fernandes

4. "Ibid."

5. "Ibid."

6. British Humanist Association

Other Evangelism Books From Spirit of Revival Evangelism

One to One Evangelism-*How to become an effective Witness for Christ*

Power Evangelism-*using the Gifts of the Holy Spirit in Evangelism*

Spirit of Revival Evangelism
Birmingham
West Midlands
Tel: 07435 000419
www.spirtiandword.org.uk